100 Bigfoot Nights

Christine D. Parker

In Dedication

To my cousin Christine, you have overcome the most challenging obstacles in your life. Your constant strength and endurance shows me that, if you hang in there long enough, miracles are possible and hope is just around the corner.

Contents

Audio Recordings

Audio recordings are available at YouTube ("100BigfootNights") or our website 100BigfootNights.com. The book sounds are listed by chapter with "Book 1" in the title.

Chapter 5 Audio - Crying 1, Mimic 1, Foxy's Warning, Working 1, Loud Whistle, Bird Whistles, Sniffing 1, Rattling 1, Clicking, Scream 1
Chapter 6 Audio - Mimic 2, Language 1, Chase part 1, Chase part 2, Chase Voice
Chapter 8 Audio - Three Yells
Chapter 10 Audio - Growl with Swishing Sound
Chapter 12 Audio - Mimic 3
Chapter 14 Audio - Mimic 4
Chapter 15 Audio - Response, Response Vocal Cries, Response Whispering Voices

There are also additional bonus sounds on YouTube and our website. We recommend using headphones when listening.

About the Author

This book is a true story, when you read it you will find for the most part we are a typical American family. I have been a housewife for most of my life and grew up in California. At a young age I joined the Army and that's where I met my husband.

Over the years we have been through the most common struggles in life. Maybe even more than most, since we moved around a lot as military families usually do. I spent most of my time involved with the schools our three sons attended and even sat on a school board once. Our sons are our biggest accomplishments in life and make us extremely proud.

When my husband finally retired, after 30 years of military service, it meant no more moving around unless we wanted too. My husband and I were finally able to buy a home and make it our own—no more living in base housing. We bought the worst house in the neighborhood because it was what we could afford. It was really destroyed (maybe now we know why). With the house in desperate need of renovation, I learned construction and we did most of the work ourselves. It took us six years but when we finished everything finally seemed perfect—or so we thought.

Acknowledgments

None of this would be possible without the love and support of my family and especially my husband. He has kept me grounded throughout this ordeal and continues to be my knight in shining armor. He has spent many days and nights by my side. He is the only one that makes me feel safe enough to continue documenting these creatures.

I wish to thank our sons whose lives are also affected. They too have been a great support and have made possible for these events to be placed on the internet. Our youngest has not only helped me to tell the story but he has also worked to design the website and edit the video clips and audio recordings. His work has been truly impressive and I'm grateful for all his help. Our middle son also understands the importance of telling our story. He has been the most affected by the Bigfoots after seeing them eye to eye a few times. He has greatly contributed to the book and maybe more than he wanted to. And, lastly, our oldest son is the reason you are able to read our story. Due to his heading of everything involved I was able to focus on writing and organizing the media.

I would also like to thank my parents. To this day they are a great means of support. My mother helps me to cope with what we are going through and offers advice. My father has been the greatest inspiration in the book's completion. He has encouraged me during the darkest of times to continue to write. He kept saying people would be interested in what's happening. I would have given up a long time ago if it wasn't for him and his much needed words of encouragement.

To my brother, who would gladly take my place in dealing with these beasts, thank you for listening to me and having a unique understanding of what we are going through. Our lives have been greatly affected and your understanding means a lot to us, as well as your advice.

To my father's girlfriend, my Aunt, and of course my cousin, Christine, thank you for calling to check on us. It's nice to know we have a lot of family support.

I would also like to thank our Bigfoot expert. He shows a true concern for our family and is only a phone call away. We are very grateful for all his help and advice.

Another important person involved in the project was Ms. Rose. She is the book cover illustrator and a talented young artist. We were very pleased.

100 Bigfoot Nights

A Chilling True Story

1

The Unforgettable Howl

Halloween decorations

It all started with a howl, and to this day, we regret having heard it. It was fall of 2012—October 13, to be exact—when my husband, Dean, decided it was time to set up our traditional Halloween display. He spent the day decorating the front yard with our Halloween décor, which consisted of a graveyard, a blow-up hearse, ghosts, and many skeletons. We always added to our display each year, and this year it was an eight-foot inflatable tree with a ghost attached and glowing bones for the graveyard. Dean decided to place the inflatable tree on the front porch so it looked like the ghost and ghoulish tree were attacking the house. It was late afternoon by the time he finished, and I went outside to see it. As usual, Dean did a wonderful job but needed to wait for nightfall to finish the display.

That evening, I was enjoying the warmth of being inside, cuddled on the couch while watching my favorite television show. Dean decided to finish the outside lighting. He had several large spotlights that needed to be adjusted to enhance the special effects. Throwing on his camouflaged coat, he headed outside. Fifteen minutes later, he came back into the house, leaned over to me, and asked, "Do you want to hear something really strange coming from the forest?"

Curious, I replied, "What is it?"

"It's something I've never heard before."

"Well, what does it sound like?" I asked, not wanting to go out into the cold.

"It's hard to explain. Just come outside and hear it," he replied with the strangest look on his face.

Intrigued, I had to go outside. I've never known Dean to be without words to describe something—it had to be bizarre. On our way to the front door, Dean retrieved and loaded one of his pistols, which was rather alarming.

As we walked across the front porch, I immediately heard what Dean could not describe—a bellowing, mournful howl coming from the forest across the street. It was a sound I too, had never heard before—an emotional howl of great despair and tragedy, in a pitch so loud it engulfed the forest, making it difficult to pinpoint its origin. We walked toward the driveway and stood by the back of our car nearest the forest. Two more howls resonated as we stared into the abyss of the woods. When it finally stopped, we were stunned, standing in the dark, listening to the silence.

I whispered, "What the hell was that?"

He said, "It's not a coyote or a dog. I don't recognize it. What do you think it is?"

I agreed it was not one of those animals, yet it was an animal. None came to mind, but, whatever it was; it was in great pain and sounded close. After a few more minutes of listening to silence and not having any kind of explanation, I blurted out, "Well, it must be some kind of hurt animal, and it's howling because it's trapped or injured." I tried logically to explain it.

Dean must have seen something when he went outside, so I asked him what happened, and he told me. He was sitting in the middle of our front lawn, about ten feet from the street, adjusting the main spotlight, when he heard the howl. It came from the forest behind him, and at first he brushed it off as his mind and ears deceiving him until it bellowed once more.

He said, "I turned around and looked at the forest, and I didn't see anything. I stopped what I was doing to listen and watch for movement. Then it happened again. I knew something was not right about the howl; it was so loud, and I couldn't recognize it. It sounded close, so I stood up and started moving toward the front door, wishing I had my pistol on me. It howled two more times as I crossed the front porch to get into the house. I kept my eyes on the forest the whole time but nothing moved. I went to get you because I couldn't identify it and I thought, 'Christine's got to hear this.'"

"What do you think it is?" I asked, wanting some type of answer.

"I don't know, but I'm going to find out," he said as he opened the car door and reached in to press the button to open the garage door to get a flashlight.

I followed him but went into the house and yelled for our youngest son, Jack, to help us. He's twenty-two years old. I told him there was an injured animal howling in the forest and we were going to search for it. Jack, being the animal lover that he is, quickly came downstairs and grabbed a flashlight, eager to help any way he could. With flashlights in hand, we all crossed the street and headed toward the forest path. We were somewhat cautious but far too curious not to follow up on the unknown animal howl.

Dean and I cautiously entered the forest only a few feet while Jack, who was told something was injured, ran deep down the forest path until we could no longer see the light of his flashlight. An eerie silence befell the forest. We could hear only the sounds of our footsteps as we walked through the leaves, weaving our flashlights back and forth looking for any signs of movement. The smell of autumn leaves, dirt, and pine nettles filled the air around us with whiffs of an unknown odor. Suddenly, I stopped. I had a weird feeling of being watched. I quickly realized this was a mistake as my thoughts turned to Jack and his disappearance deep into the darkness. Fearing for his safety, I yelled for him but could hear only a faint reply somewhere down the path. I expressed to Dean my need to leave the woods and to call for Jack to come back. He did, and Jack returned, to my relief.

I convinced them it was too dark and too uncertain to continue searching the woods. We came out of the forest and back on to the street. Jack asked what was wrong; he sensed my concern as I stood quietly staring at the forest with my arms crossed. I explained to him that something strange was happening; the forest should not have been that quiet. Now disturbed by the howl, Dean and I stood in the street and discussed it while Jack paced along the forest front, shining his flashlight into it and hoping the animal would howl again.

We saw the headlights from a car as it came around the corner; it drove slowly and stopped in front of us. It was our next-door neighbors Mike; his wife, Carla; and their daughter, Sara, on their way home from dinner. They stopped to ask what we were doing standing in the street. We told them we heard a strange howl coming from the forest but couldn't explain what animal made it. We talked for a few minutes, and they wished us luck and went home. It was very dark and chilly, so after an hour or so, we decided to go back into the house, even though we had no answers—only a mystery to solve.

What type of animal could make such a disturbing howl so close to our home? It was a haunting question about a howl so deep and emotional it would make a baritone opera singer envious. Something large was bellowing from the forest, and I was determined to find out what it was.

The next day, I went online to search for the unidentified animal that howled in the forest. After a few hours of searching the internet and listening to many animal howls, I became frustrated and wanted to give up. Jack noticed I was exasperated, so he came into the office to help. I described to him again the intense magnitude of the howl and even tried desperately to mimic it. He began to search the web while I sat on the couch across from him, exhausted from my futile searches. He played a wide range of animal howls and kept asking whether they matched. I would say louder, deeper, or no. After many tries, he finally played a recording and said, "Listen to this mournful howl."

I listened, and to my surprise, he had found it—it was a match, but the only difference was the howl we heard was much louder and clearer! I jumped from the couch with a huge smile on my face, wanting to give him a big hug and kiss.

Relieved and thrilled to finally have an answer, I yelled, "You found it! What kind of animal is it?"

He had a curious look on his face and hesitantly said, "A recording of a Bigfoot in Ohio, in 1994."

His words hit me like a ton of bricks. My joy turned to complete shock as I struggled to make sense of it. I couldn't believe what he had just said, so I immediately asked whether he was kidding.

He replied, "I'm not joking; it's a Bigfoot howl."

I hurried to the computer in disbelief to see whether the recording was legit. Numb, I just stood there, staring at the computer as he played the howl repeatedly.

Completely bewildered, I asked, "What made you think of a Bigfoot?"

Jack said he was getting tired of me saying no to every howl so he played the Bigfoot one as a last resort. It kept coming up on the search engine when he typed in animal moans and howls, among other things. I knew what he was referring to because I too had seen it when I searched, but I ignored it because it seemed outrageous. He searched for other Bigfoot howls and played them too, but the Ohio 1994 howl was the closest match.

I felt light-headed and had to sit down as my mind raced through the events from the previous night. In order to verify the howl, we quickly called Dean into the office so he could hear it. Jack played the howl for him twice.

Dean listened very carefully and answered, "Yes, that's it, except the one I heard was louder. Great, you found it! What type of animal is it?"

Jack told him, and Dean just stood there staring at us for a moment. I think he thought we were joking.

I was speechless and didn't know what to say.

He said, "Well, that's what it sounded like," as he left the room to finish what he was doing.

I don't know exactly what he was thinking, but it was nearly impossible to believe a Bigfoot was across the street. I thought, "A Bigfoot? What the hell? Are you kidding?" This revelation was more than I could handle. I felt like my ears were going to explode, so I told Jack not to play it anymore. He could clearly see this was very disturbing to me, so he left the room and went upstairs, happy that he finally heard the incredible howl.

I sat in the office for a while, thinking this could not be happening and there was no way it could be true. Bigfoots don't live in a suburban neighborhood literally five minutes from the main street of town and the freeway. We didn't live high up in the mountains where they are sighted. Yes, our home was on a corner at the end of the street and there was a forest across from us, but a Bigfoot? How ridiculous.

After my initial shock came the denial as I tried to reason with myself. The internet recording in Ohio was supposed to be a Bigfoot howling, but how does anyone really *know*? It could be some other unidentified creature. Just because they say it is, does that make it true? Not wanting to believe, I struggled to reason with it, but I had no other explanation for the howl, and no matter how hard I tried, I couldn't explain it away.

As I began to accept the possibility, I thought how ironic it all seemed because my entire fear of the forest had been based on Bigfoots. I had spent my whole life trying to avoid running into one. I always believed in their existence and had an unnatural fear of them. I refused to go camping, walking, or driving on dark roads surround by forest because I was deathly afraid of them lurking in it.

When Dean returned to the office, I asked him what he thought about it.

He said, "Well, I guess there's a Bigfoot across the street."

I nearly lost it and became emotional. He basically said the wrong thing. I wanted his reassurance that there was not a Bigfoot in the forest—not to mention he seemed disinterested! He quickly realized my concern and sat quietly as I again tried desperately to convince myself this was not true. He listened for a while, tried to comfort me, by agreeing to everything I said and then we went to bed. Dean and I have been married thirty years, so he knew how to reassure me.

I couldn't really blame Dean for not feeling the way I did. He was retired Army, so he had seen and done a lot and little surprised him anymore. In the military, he held many positions that involved being in the forest after dark. As a child, he went camping every summer, and he had hunted in the past. He obviously was not afraid of the forest or even a Bigfoot being in it. Needless to say, he had no problem sleeping—unlike me.

2

The Creepy Forest

Forest pathway

The next morning I was in a complete daze as I stood in the office downstairs and stared out the window at the forest across the street. It appeared quite colorful, engulfed in a ray of autumn colors with tall trees, bushes, and vines. There were squirrels jumping along the forest bottom and playing innocently within the fallen leaves. Overall, the forest added a little nature to our lives and should have been relaxing to anyone living across from it, but for me, this was not the case. The forest appeared somewhat normal during the day, but at night it transformed into a dark place where strange shadows lurked. All my creepy feelings about the forest came rushing back along with the disturbing memories from years past.

I could view the forest from the office and dining room widows at the front of our house, as well as from the second-floor master bedroom and our son Adam's room. We also had a small window off the family room that sat across from it. The land the forest sat on was quite large and they couldn't build houses on it because of all the water drainage from our housing track. Behind the part that faced the street the forest continued for miles, I assumed, with a creek running through it. Directly across the street from our mailbox, to the right of the driveway, was an entrance pathway into the forest. Our house was a corner house at the end of our housing development.

Immediately next-door, past our driveway to the left of our house, was Mike and Carla's house. Directly across from them and next to the forest was Steve and Becky's house. After their houses, the neighborhood continued, with homes on both sides of the street. However, the backyards of the homes behind Steve and Becky's house, on the forest side, were up against the woods. Past our house to the right of the forest front, a house sat alone on that corner facing an adjoining street. The forest wrapped behind that corner neighbor's house, Mr. Drake's. Across his street was another set of houses that bordered a large park (see illustration at the end of chapter).

We purchased our home seven years earlier when Dean retired. We were so excited to buy our home that not much thought was ever given to the woods. Although there were times,

I often wondered whether transients were residing in the forest. Outside I would sense someone in the forest watching us and hear weird sounds of mumbled voices. I'm originally from a large city, so having people living on a vacant piece of land is not uncommon. I figured they were just passing through and eventually would leave. We were so preoccupied with renovating the house I really didn't have time to dwell on the strange sounds or the people in the forest—not to mention I wasn't going to investigate any dark shadows that were moving—so I decided to ignore them.

However, as the years passed, it made no sense—why would people be staying in the forest in complete darkness, especially during the wintertime when it was freezing cold? It seemed illogically, yet there was a presence in the forest at certain times, I just couldn't explain it. I also couldn't explain the strong feelings I had of someone lurking in the darkness. Coming home late at night, I sensed times when we were not alone. I remember standing on the porch in the dark, waiting for Dean to open the front door, and feeling I wasn't the only one standing behind him. Sometimes when we arrived home late at night, I would look at the forest and see the dark shadows moving or strange silhouettes of someone standing by a tree. Reflecting back, I get the chills thinking about what it could have been.

Even more unnerving to me were the times Dean would park the vehicles across the street next to the forest with the passenger side on the easement, a ten-foot area of grass and weeds before the forest started. I would cringe having to get in the vehicle at night. Crossing the street, I could feel conscious eyes watching me and see suspiciously darker areas in the thicket, slightly moving. The moment my foot touched grass, the forest would become completely still and silent. I would get an eerie feeling, and instinctively place my head down, not wanting to look into the forest, for fear of what I might see. Standing with my back to the forest while waiting for Dean to unlock the door, I would sense someone standing behind me. Once open, I would quickly jump in the vehicle and lock it as fast as I could and then shake off the creepy feeling.

I often told Dean about these feelings and the dark moving shadows in the forest, but he knew I had a fear of the woods and thought maybe that was what was happening. Sometimes I thought maybe he was right and I was being too sensitive, because not everyone in the house felt that way. When home from college, our oldest son, William, often placed food in the forest for the wild animals to eat, and so did Jack. They were not afraid of the forest and still sometimes went in it after dark against my wishes. On the other hand, our middle son, Adam, wouldn't go anywhere near the forest. He often arrived home late from work and parked in the street across from it.

He would tell us, "I get a weird feeling when I exit my truck, like someone's watching me. It's creepy because the hair on my arms and neck stands up. Some nights I can't get into the house fast enough, and I hear strange noises."

I too had heard other strange noises at night, such as banging, knocking, and screaming, so I knew what he meant. These sounds only added to my fear of the forest and the animals in it. However the most perplexing sounds over the years were the ones close to our house or up against it.

One year, in particular, I remember a strange scratching sound that to this day still bothers me. It would happen in the wee hours of the morning while I was alone in the office. It would start out scratching slowly at random intervals, and then get louder over a period of several minutes. It scratched high up on the wall just to the right of the desk, at the exterior siding. That particular wall formed part of a cove on the front porch where we had an outdoor table set. I couldn't see in the cove from the window, so it was pointless to look out. I often had the feeling that something was trying to get my attention because of the way it scratched. I figured it had to be some type of animal but reflecting back, what type of animal could scratch a wall at the six foot level with nothing below it but siding?

There was also the year our trash cans disappeared I remember it because we had to file a police report before our trash company would replace them. Our trash cans were quite large, with hinged tops and wheels on the bottom. They sat on the side of our house next to the family room. Some nights I would repeatedly hear our trash can tops being lifted and then dropped and the cans being bumped together. After hearing these sounds repeatedly, sometimes I would turn on the side porch light and look out the window, but see nothing out of place. It happened so often, that as the months passed, I stopped looking out the window, and ultimately blamed the raccoons. Until one day, all three trash cans went missing. It made no sense why anyone would steal trash cans full of trash. Even more disturbing was how they did it. Our trash cans sat quite a distance from the street, in near complete darkness, and they were heavy, requiring you to wheel them one at a time. Dean and our sons did this every trash day. It made a lot of noise and also left wheel tracks across the front lawn. Whoever took them did so without a sound that night and left no wheel tracks.

The next day after filing the police report, we installed motion sensor lights around the house. The lights would be off during the day and dimmed from dusk until dawn. When detecting motion, they would become brighter, illuminating the house. I also insisted that the house be locked at all times, including the windows. In the South, this was somewhat uncommon; most of our neighbors left everything unlocked. But someone was approaching our house at night and we thought, maybe these lights would detour them.

Only one time, do I remember seeing something strange coming from the forest? It kept bothering our oldest dog, Foxy, she is now fifteen-years-old and a Chow-Chow mix. When she was younger, she would lay with her snout on the window ledge in the dining room, the ledge was one foot off the ground, to the right of the front door. She would lay there for hours at night staring at the forest across the street. Sometimes in the early hours of the morning, she would bark loudly and aggressively. It would often wake us up since our bedroom on the second floor sat directly above the dining room. We would come downstairs, to see what she was barking at, turn on all the outside lighting and look, but not see anything. At first we thought maybe, she was just barking at the rabbits on the front lawn, but it was the way she barked, with her hackles standing up and snapping at the air, that made us think otherwise. So we continued the check every time she barked, some nights we would become frustrated because she wouldn't stop even after we checked and went back to bed. This kept happening over and over until one night I decided to look out the upstairs window the minute she started to bark and I saw a strange looking animal.

It emerged from the forest path and walked awkwardly on all fours. It had large upper shoulders; long weird-looking front legs; and a sloped back— like a hyena. I watched it in the moonlight from our bedroom window as it walked along the easement toward Mr. Drake's house. It was the shape and the way it walked that made it strange looking. I kept trying to see its face to identify the animal, but it was walking away moving at a slow, steady pace.

The next morning I told Dean and our sons about it. They kept saying hyenas didn't live here and ignored the description. Not knowing what it was, I searched the internet for similar-looking animals in the state but found nothing. Eventually, I gave up, and after months of Foxy barking and not knowing what to do, we finally placed a piece of furniture in front of the window so she couldn't see out anymore.

Around the fifth year of living in our home, I felt the need for security cameras in the front of the house. Strangely, I felt uneasy during the day, home alone, as well as at night when alone in the office. It really made no sense, but I kept having feelings of being stalked. Also, Foxy seemed nervous during the day as well as at night, sometimes barking near the front door while pacing back and forth. Dean wanted me to feel safe, so he installed two exterior cameras and placed the monitor in the office. This allowed me watch them anytime I wanted to. One of the cameras was installed over the top of the garage, and it could view the driveway and some of the street in front of the house with the forest in the background. The other one was to the left of the front door, focused on the area in front of it so I could see whether someone was standing there. I mostly used them during the day and occasionally at night. Although they were not night vision cameras, they could view the lit areas. However, there were a lot of blind spots, such as the cove on the front porch.

These cameras also were equipped with microphones but they were usually turned off.

Although the cameras had helped over the past two years since we installed them, my unsettling feelings never went away. Logically thinking that the house was safe from intruders, what more could we do?

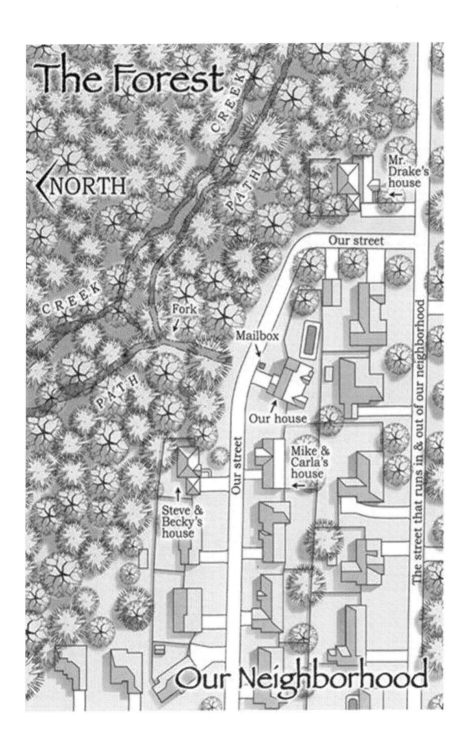

The Forest

CREEK

NORTH

PATH

Mr. Drake's house

CREEK

Fork

Mailbox

Our street

Our house

Our street

Mike & Carla's house

The street that runs in & out of our neighborhood

PATH

Steve & Becky's house

Our Neighborhood

3

Foxy's Warning

FOXY, ROCKY, HEIDI

As I thought about our situation, I kept wondering what we should do. We were the only ones aware that there was a beast in the forest—perhaps a Bigfoot. What about the safety of other families in the neighborhood? What should we do?

After doing some research on the internet, I found a website of an organization that investigated Bigfoot sightings. You filed a report online about the incident and they contacted you. I assumed those people running this reporting website would know what to do, such as warn families in the area or remove the Bigfoot. At the very least, I figured the organization might already have an ongoing investigation in the area and this information could help to solve another mystery. I convinced Dean that filing a report with them was the responsible thing to do no matter how unbelievable it sounded. After submitting a report, I really didn't know whether anyone would respond because it was just a howl and not a sighting.

In the meantime, my fear was getting the best of me as the haunting howl continued to echo in my mind. I was unable to ignore that a Bigfoot could be living across the street. Just the thought of one nearby was turning my world upside down. Night after sleepless night, I would sit in the office while watching the monitor and listening to the microphones. I could no longer watch television or enjoy anything after dark. Every little noise during the night made me uneasy, and I was afraid to let our dogs outside.

One night on the monitor, I saw our next-door neighbor Mike going into the woods with a flashlight. Mike was very tall and thin, so I easily recognized him. Fearing for his safety, I jumped up and flew outside to stop him. I caught him just before he entered the forest and asked him whether he saw something in the woods.

He said, "No, I was just looking for my cat. She's been missing for a while."

Without a thought, I felt compelled to warn him, so I revealed that we suspected a Bigfoot was in the forest and that he should not go in there, especially at night.

He politely laughed and said, "Well, I don't know," as he looked away, shinning his flashlight into the forest. Mike was from Texas and an avid hunter, so he obviously was not fearful of the woods.

I reminded him of the night we heard the howl, and he remembered us standing in the street. As unbelievable as the words sounded coming out of my mouth, I told him that we thought it was a Bigfoot because we had found the same howl on the internet and it was of a Bigfoot howling in Ohio. I informed him that we filed a report of the incident to a Bigfoot organization online and told him not to say anything to anyone in the neighborhood until we had more information. He seemed uncomfortable as he stood there, still shining his flashlight into the forest.

He said, "Well, you know there are raccoons, coyotes, and deer in the forest?" I shook my head yes. He continued, "The raccoons and coyotes make noises at night all the time, and maybe that's what you heard."

I replied, "No, I'm positive it was not a raccoon or coyote. Believe me, I wish it were that simple."

"Oh, well, got to go tell the wife," he said as he walked away in haste.

Standing outside alone in the dark it dawned on me how insane I must have sounded. I felt humiliated and thought of how all the years of them knowing me to be a logical, and sane person just went out the window. I knew something like this could happen if I told anyone since it did sound ridiculous. Dean had warned of this, yet it did not stop me from warning Mike—I was too concerned for his safety. At this point I could only imagine what he was thinking or telling Carla, his wife.

Now I understood the conflict people must go through in similar situations. They see or hear something unexplainable and decide to tell others, only to get brushed off as being imaginative, crazy or seeking attention. It's a difficult position to be in, sacrificing your credibility based on a howl and an instinct, even though it may or may not be true.

Over the next few nights, I saw Mike going in and out of the woods with a flashlight. It was terrifying to watch him even though I figured he was looking for his cat and was concerned about her. With nothing more I could do, I just watched and held my breath, hoping nothing bad would happen to him.

On Saturday morning, October 20, the phone rang. A man said, "Hello, I'm a Bigfoot investigator and saw your online report. I live nearby and was wondering whether I could come over and interview you."

Thrilled, I said, "That would be just fine."

Finally, an expert to tell us there was no way a Bigfoot could be in the forest and I would be able to sleep at night again—or so I hoped. Within an hour, he was at our house to interview us.

He was an older gentleman with glasses, very thin and fit. He wore a plaid outdoor shirt, light-colored pants and hiking boots. He had a camera around his neck and a writing pad in his hand. After exchanging pleasantries, he briefed us regarding his background. He specialized in tracking and evidence collection. He was retired from his job and had been investigating Bigfoot cases for about twenty-five years part-time while he worked and now full-time. He was assisting the online organization with its investigations, but because of his age, he no longer wanted to travel out of state. He took only the local cases in the area (in this story I will refer to him as Mr. Hill).

He began to ask us a few questions. He noticed we had a lot of dogs. In addition to our oldest dog, Foxy, we have a ten-year-old Cockapoo (also named Cockapoo) and two one-year-old pups. The male pup, Rocky, is a Lab mix, and the female pup, Heidi, is a Shepherd mix. He asked about any strange behavior from them. Since the pups were new additions to the family and we only had them a few months. We told him about Foxy's past years of barking at night in the house by the front window. He asked what time she usually barked. We stated between 2:00 and 3:00 a.m. He found this very interesting.

I told him about the night she barked when I saw the strange animal that resembled a hyena coming from the forest. I was reluctant to tell him because it seemed ridiculous, but he was interested and asked more questions about the shape and how it walked.

I said, "It wasn't a Bigfoot because it walked on all fours."

He replied, "Bigfoots do mimic other animals, and people often describe them as looking like hyenas when on all fours due to their high shoulders and sloping back. They do this because if people see them, they believe they're some other type of animal."

I found this to be noteworthy because after seeing that strange animal, I had no idea what it was or to whom to report it.

He asked whether anyone had been putting food in the forest. We explained that over the years our sons William and Jack had placed leftovers in the forest for a family of raccoons and rabbits at least once a week. However, with the two of them independently doing this, it could have been more often. They would rather put food in the forest than in the trash because they didn't like to waste. Something was eating the food, and they did not really know what they were feeding, but since it was always gone, they were happy.

He shook his head and said, "You would be surprised how many people do that thinking they're feeding little critters and it turns out they have been feeding something else. Why, in this neighborhood alone, I wonder how many people are putting food in the forest."

We informed him that our next-door neighbors Mike and Carla often placed bowls of food on their front porch to feed the raccoons and stray cats. He shook his head again and smiled.

We all went outside to illustrate where we were standing and what Dean was doing when the howling started. After hearing our story, Mr. Hill asked whether he could take pictures of the Halloween decorations.

When Dean turned on the display, Mr. Hill smiled and said, "I know why you heard the howling that night. It looks like something terrible happened at your house, with all the skeletons and ghosts and that inflatable tree on your porch. The Bigfoot didn't know what to make of it. He thought something bad happened to the family, thus the mournful howl. They are very sensitive to their surroundings, and this upset him."

I explained that we had always set up a Halloween display and added to it every year. Evidently, this year our new additions must have upset the creature.

I told Dean, "Great job, you scared a Bigfoot."

Dean replied, "Well, I wanted to scare something."

"How insane is this?" I thought to myself.

After taking a few pictures, Mr. Hill said he was going to take a look in the forest and would be back to talk with us. When he returned, he told us he found Bigfoot tracks traveling along the creek. He was trying to figure out whether the Bigfoot was just traveling through there or also bedding down nearby.

I asked whether he was sure, hoping for even the slightest possibility that it was not a Bigfoot, and he replied, "You heard the howl; nothing can howl like that other than a Bigfoot."

As we sat in the office, he began to inform us about Bigfoots. He told many stories and showed us official reports on the internet that he had written and investigated; there were a lot of cases over the years, and his accounts were fascinating. I was most impressed by his memory of places, times, and events. He knew all about Bigfoots and informed us that they were smart, neat, and patient.

Online, he pulled up a satellite map of our home that showed the forest and the surrounding area. He explained in detail what would draw a Bigfoot to our neighborhood. Our forest had a freshwater creek that connected to a larger lake, houses with sheds in the forest for shelter, wild game, berries, and probably many people feeding it. If you traveled southeast, there was a city dump, old mines, railroad tracks, and a larger forest. All were less than ten miles from our house, which was nothing for a Bigfoot to travel in one day.

He said, "They like to travel along the railroad tracks because the sound of the trains can drown out their vocals. They howl to each other when the train's whistle blows. They are very territorial, and this must be part of a male's area." He mentioned to us that he was tracking a group just south of here and wondered whether this Bigfoot was part of that group.

He continued, "People feed them all the time, year after year." He named several states where this had happened—not just ours. He described the most common type in the area as having long reddish-brown hair and being eight to ten feet tall with a human-looking face. During his investigations, he had seen many and said they were very humanlike. We were amazed at how much he knew about them, and I was especially perplexed by his lack of fear.

He looked down at our dog, Foxy. She was lying on the office floor and quietly sleeping. The pups were outside, and Cockapoo was there as well. He asked us what type of dog she was and whether she was the one that barked in the house. We told him yes, she was the one barking at night, and we believed she was a Chow-Chow mix. He commented on how she appeared to have wolf in her. Foxy may have had wolf in her because she was a rescue dog found in the forest way north of here and she weighed 120 pounds.

I mentioned her strange outdoor barking at night as well. In a constant annoying pattern with no real purpose other than to announce her presence. Sometimes when she did this bark, she pounced with her front legs and acted aggressive. What was strange about it was that she stayed on the porch in the backyard, barking and snapping at the air, but she didn't go near the fence. We spent many years trying to break her of this habit because she did it late at night after wanting to go outside.

He said, "She knows the Bigfoot is out there. She is doing what I call a 'booger bark'—she is barking because she senses it nearby. She hears or smells him, but she can't see him, so she is giving a warning bark. It is very different from an attack bark when she sees something."

I told him that after she did this bark, she banged at the back door, wanting to come inside quickly. He said she knew there was danger and she was smart to do that.

He told us that he would return to place some bait and maybe record sounds. He was also going to check for footprints south of us near the railroad crossing. We all agreed that a Bigfoot in a housing area must be handled carefully to avoid panic in the neighborhood. Dean and I did not want this situation to get out of hand, so we asked him whether he could leave our address out of the official report, and he agreed to do so.

After his visit, the reality of the situation became clear. It was a lot of information to process, and Mr. Hill seemed very credible. Unfortunately for us, he basically confirmed that a Bigfoot was in the woods and we had no choice in the matter.

4

Signs

Bigfoot footprint in dried mud

The next day, Mr. Hill returned to continue his investigation. He informed us that he had found Bigfoot prints south of us by the railroad crossing. His plan was to set up some bait and sit in the forest at nightfall to meet the Bigfoot and record some sounds. At first I thought he was kidding but soon realized he was serious; evidently, he did this when investigating Bigfoot cases.

Before setting up the bait, Dean and I ventured into the forest with Mr. Hill, who found many signs indicating Bigfoot activity, such as trees that were peeled along one side. He said, "They strip the bark from the trees when hiding behind them." He looked up, and grabbed a broken tree branch that was still attached, dangling high up over our heads. He said, "They like to twist the top of the branches almost completely off, yet leave them still attached by a strip of bark," as he pulled it down because it was dangerous to walk under. There were also other signs such as, snapped limbs or trees broken in half and some that were simply pushed over. I agreed that something strong had to have done this since the trunks were thick and the trees were large.

He identified several tree stumps that were placed upright in a pattern yet not rooted to the ground; he stated, "This was one way they marked their territory." He also told us about a "Bigfoot warning sign" they used to warn other Bigfoots to stay away. It consisted of several branches wrapped up with vines— like a crude teepee. He said, "If we saw one, we would know what it meant." In addition, he showed us other clues that indicated something large was moving through the forest and snapping the tips of branches.

I photographed all of the evidence he pointed out while he continued to tell interesting Bigfoot stories, but my attention was elsewhere. I kept thinking, "Is this *really* happening?" As he continued to talk to Dean, I ventured through the forest; I was completely fascinated by my surroundings. Finally, I was inside the forest across the street. I had no idea it was so large. As I navigated through the many trees, the leaves made a crunching noise as I walked. There were cleared pathways through the forest, as though something was constantly using them, and I followed one. When I came upon a large mound of dirt, it gave me an eerie feeling, so I stopped to look around. I noticed two more mounds throughout the forest bottom underneath the trees. An odd feeling of great sadness came over me, as if I was standing in a graveyard. The mounds looked like shallow graves for large bodies, with the dirt piled on top. I had the impression that something was buried there from a long time ago. The mounds were covered in leaves and had branches protruding through them with upright stumps placed nearby. They reminded me of grave markers, and after seeing them, I decided it was time to leave the forest.

Dean offered to assist Mr. Hill in setting up the bait. They went farther back in the forest somewhere along the path and tied a red mesh bag filled with fried chicken high up in a tree. They seemed to be gone a long time, and it quickly became dark. I was anxiously pacing back and forth in the office while watching the monitor and listening to the forest through the camera over the garage. I had a horrible feeling this was not a good idea. Soon, Dean returned and left Mr. Hill sitting in the forest. I was a very nervous and had the phone nearby, ready to call 911 at the first sign of trouble.

At 8:30 p.m., I saw someone running towards house; shockingly, it was Jack. He was in the forest sitting with Mr. Hill. He had gone out earlier to talk with him and see how the bait was set up. He returned only because he had other things to do; otherwise, he would have stayed in the forest. Jack had no fear of Bigfoots and would have liked to meet one. I was upset with him because I didn't know he was out there sitting in the woods in the first place.

I was beginning to express concerns over him being out there when suddenly we heard a loud, threatening growl resonating from the forest. Shocked, we immediately froze and stared at the monitor as I watched and waited for something more frightening to happen. We could hear the sounds of footsteps approaching; someone was walking through the forest and crushing leaves with each step. I was anxious and fearful wondering what was happening deep down the path where Mr.

Hill was sitting. After a few tense seconds we finally saw who was exiting the forest. It was Mr. Hill.

He quickly emerged, entered his truck, turned around in our driveway, and drove slowly down the street toward Mr. Drake's house. By the way he was driving—so slowly—I thought he was in pursuit of the growling beast. I wanted to call him immediately and ask what was happening, but I thought it might hinder his chances of tracking the creature. So I decided to wait until morning, after another long, sleepless night.

Finally, morning arrived, and I called Mr. Hill to find out what had happened and why he left the forest. He said he had left because he forgot to turn off his cell phone and someone called whom he needed to speak with. Further, he explained that while sitting in the forest, he heard heavy footsteps approaching him from the creek. When his cell phone rang, he heard the footsteps stop and walk away at a slightly faster pace. Figuring his cover was blown, he decided to leave the forest and try another day.

I asked whether he heard the growl, since it happened only seconds before he left the forest.

He replied, "It was hard to hear anything other than me walking on the leaves because of the hearing device. However, I did hear something that sounded like a car engine. Well, at any rate, I hope you don't think I left because of a growl. I've had rocks and sticks thrown at me before. They will throw things, growl and puff if you get too close, and they could easily hit you with something. But they don't; it's just their way of warning you and scaring you off."

I replied, "Well it sure scared the heck out of me, but honestly, I thought you were chasing it."

He asked from what side of the forest we heard the growl, and I told him to the left of the entrance. He stated, "Makes me think there's more than one, because they will distract you from one direction while the other circles around."

"Great," I said, "so there's more than one?"

Hearing the concern in my voice, he said, "I'll be there soon to look for tracks and check the bait."

After checking the bait, Mr. Hill found that the mesh bag holding the chicken was torn and some of the pieces were missing. However, the suspects were raccoons; the bag had tiny bite marks and tears along the side. We talked as he readjusted the bait, and Dean and I offered to check on it for him and call if it was eaten. In the meantime, he went walking through the forest, and Dean and I went back into the house and awaited his return. He was gone for more than an hour, and when he came back, he seemed distracted, deep in thought. I didn't know what he was thinking or what he found, because he didn't say anything to us. He had other cases he was working on at the time and had to leave, but again he said he would return.

Later that afternoon, Jack and William decided to set up some experiments of their own. Mr. Hill had told Jack that Bigfoots enjoyed peanut butter and shiny or colorful stones and didn't like to make messes. They decided to lay down pennies and quarters, all heads up, and set down five polished stones on the trail in a cross-shaped pattern. They tied food high up in a tree and placed chips on the ground and left. It was completely dark when they finished, and I was concerned about them being in the forest so late.

After their excursion, William explained to me what they did in the forest and also mentioned a putrid odor. He said, "It smelled so bad out there I had a hard time concentrating on setting up the experiments. It stunk like sewage. I didn't say anything to Jack because I know he can't smell." (Jack has a medical condition called anosmia.)

I found this to be very interesting because earlier Mr. Hill had told us a story about two police officers who chased a Bigfoot. William was not there during this conversation, so he couldn't have known anything about it.

Mr. Hill had said they chased the Bigfoot into a steep drainage ditch on the side of a road. One officer jumped into the narrow ditch to follow the creature but became violently ill from its "sewage stench" and had to go to a hospital. I told Mr. Hill I thought maybe Bigfoots put off a stench when they were anxious, like a skunk, and he just smiled.

The next morning, Dean and I checked on Mr. Hill's bait, but nothing was disturbed; it was still hanging in the tree. We looked around, found nothing, and left. Later that day, Jack went to check on his and William's experiments. All of their food had been eaten, and not even a crumb from the chips was left. One of the polished stones was moved two inches from its original position, and one of the quarters was turned with tails facing up and then placed back in the same spot. Jack took photos of the stones and coins to verify their positions, and he was excited by their results. He concluded that someone had consciously looked at the quarter, turned it around, and placed it back—someone with fingers. However, again he had been in the forest after dark, and this upset me, so I told him to please stay out of the forest and reminded him that Mr. Hill would handle the investigation.

I really didn't want him feeding the Bigfoots anymore because I wanted the creatures to leave. I told Jack we were not feeding four dogs and two Bigfoots everyday—that was ridiculous. Of course, he didn't listen to me because I found out later that he continued to place packages of crackers and microwaved burritos high up in the trees, only to have them eaten overnight. No wonder why Mr. Hill's bait was not touched and after a few days he cut it down because it was rotting. Mr. Hill replaced it with red potatoes and said Bigfoots like to eat them, but still nothing touched it.

I understood Jack's interest in wanting to perform his own experiments, and everyone seemed to be aware that he was doing this except me. Mr. Hill had even given him some suggestions regarding his bait. I didn't want my fear to stand in the way of progress, but I also didn't want Jack in the forest after dark since Mr. Hill mentioned that Bigfoots were mostly nocturnal. So, after a long, involved conversation, Jack and I came to an agreement regarding his experiments, and I reluctantly agreed to check his bait traps during the day when he was gone. Mr. Hill would also monitor the situation by checking the evidence if we found any.

Jack, Dean, and I went into the forest to see where Jack had been placing the food. It was to the right of the forest entrance, approximately forty feet in, near Mr. Drake's house on a narrow pathway parallel to the creek. It was on the opposite side from where Mr. Hill was placing food. I thought Mr. Hill was placing the food farther in the forest along the path to draw the Bigfoots away from the street. However, Mr. Hill had no problem going deep into the forest, whereas I did, and this spot was far enough for me; also in this location along the forest bottom were patches of mud and cleared leaves, caused by the rainwater as it made its way to the creek. We all agreed this was a good spot to hopefully get footprints.

Over the next several weeks, Jack began trying different experiments. He placed food high in the trees, tied by strings, and sometimes underneath he would sweep the forest floor to clear leaves and then soak the ground to create mud to capture footprints. He put a giant colorful rock weighing about five pounds on a fallen tree trunk. He found pushed-over stumps and placed them upright in a pattern. On top of one of the stumps he also placed a ten-inch plush monkey to see whether it would go missing.

The plush monkey lasted a week and was never seen again. Sometimes it would take a few days, but a Bigfoot did seem to be eating the food and knocking over the stumps, as well as breaking more branches. Also, the heavy rock was moved two feet from the tree trunk. Sometimes we would find what appeared to be Bigfoot tracks—barefoot feet with flared toes on the edges of the mud. When possible, I would contact Mr. Hill to verify the footprints. Walking through the forest, he used Popsicle sticks to mark the heel and toes and tried to follow them. However, he said they took extreme measures not to leave tracks for anyone to follow. He had knowledge of some even using a branch with leaves to brush away their own footprints. When Mr. Hill was unavailable, we also took our own photographs of what we thought were footprints.

In order to photograph footprints, it was paramount to check the forest first thing in the morning before the leaves fell and covered them. If the weather was bad or windy, it hindered the investigation. When possible, our routine consisted of checking the bait in the tree and photographing any evidence. Dean and I would normally preform this task, but sometimes it was just me having to face my fear of the forest.

First, I would stand facing the forest and peek into it to make sure nothing was blatantly standing there. I would begin my slow descent deeper into the woods, but I took time after each step to scan the surroundings and listen for movement, before taking another. I saw things that didn't make sense, such as piled leaves, branches, and pine needles. They didn't fall from the trees in that manner; someone had to be piling them. The forest had an eerie silence, and even though I was only 30 feet from the street, I could not hear anything from it—not even the cars as they drove by. Likewise, I could yell and not be heard. Sometimes I had creepy feelings of someone watching me, but ignored them to get the evidence.

I understood how people traveling alone in a forest could easily disappear, among the tall trees and thick bush. After all, who truly knows what's lurking in a forest, watching from the shadows cast by the trees? Over the years I had done a lot of stupid things in my life, but this was truly the most daring, even though it was broad daylight. There was something abnormal in the forest, and it made my skin crawl.

Finally, I would make it to the bait, and sometimes it was eaten, surrounded by broken branches and freshly dropped leaves. I would navigate around it, careful not to disturb any tracks nearby, especially the Bigfoot-looking tracks on the edges of the mud. Fearing they were still lurking, I wanted to quickly take pictures and leave. Sometimes I would take one picture and the camera would die. I would literally be straddling over a footprint, deep in the forest, and have no way to properly document it. Even though the batteries in the camera were new, it would simply shut off and indicate low batteries. This happened a few times, so I began carrying extra batteries because I only wanted to make one horrifying trip. Something in the forest was draining the batteries and carrying extra one's helped because it also happened when Dean and I were in the forest.

When we mentioned it to Jack, he recalled it happening to Mr. Hill and his recording devices too. Finding this very interesting, Dean and Jack researched the internet and found a paranormal site that explained batteries being mysteriously drained. Evidently, ghosts are the leading cause of this in order to manifest themselves. They discussed it for a while and came to the conclusion that some unexplained force was active in that part of the woods. It wouldn't surprise me if this were true because that forest was really creepy.

As Jack continued his experiments, picking up the stumps and placing food, weather permitting. Mr. Hill also stopped by to continue his investigation, and did inform us of a few things, but I can't comment on all the evidence he found or what he did during his investigation. Dean and I concluded this was common practice for the investigators to also be somewhat elusive with their findings so as not to influence the outcome. However, sometimes he would arrive and venture deep into the woods, tracking the Bigfoots for miles I assume.

One cold morning we invited Mr. Hill in for coffee and asked whether he had found anymore tracks. He said he had seen tracks of what looked like a wild pig and, interestingly, a mink and told us he had also seen evidence of a large buck traveling up and down the creek.

He paused, took another sip of coffee, and said, "I also found the footprint of a Bigfoot as it jumped across the creek. You could clearly see where it jumped the creek because it made a deep impression." Other tracks he had found in the forest were those of deer, raccoons, and coyotes, as well as a coyote dog, which had a print larger than the rest of the coyotes. He told us it was common for coyote packs to tail Bigfoots.

"The coyotes are looking for a few scraps from the Bigfoots kills," he explained. "The Bigfoots don't mind as long as they stay quiet during the hunt. But if the coyotes make too much noise, they will run them down, catch one, and skin it alive to teach the rest of the coyotes to be quiet. They have been known to do the same thing to dogs that bark and annoy them. They pick them up by the back of the neck, pulling their skin inside out, and throw them to the ground. Or they take a branch, or their fist, and fatally strike them in the head."

This story terrified me because I worried for our dogs, especially the pups, who liked to run around the yard at night barking and Rocky attacking anything that moved. But he said not to worry—most dogs cowered and ran from the Bigfoots. His constant reassurance to us was that we were in no present danger. I, on the other hand, kept picturing this large, strong,

Neanderthal-looking creature standing in the forest. It really disturbed me because this was not just a sighting for us—it was a perpetual presence.

5

Observant

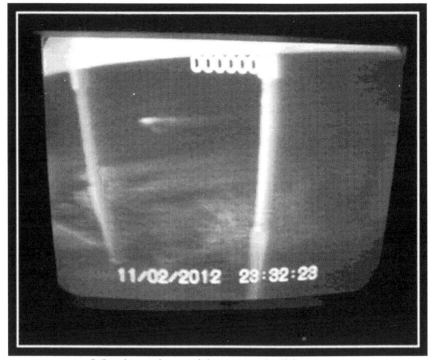

Monitor view with car parked in street

With Bigfoots nearby, I couldn't sleep at night. Most nights I would sit in the office while watching and listening to the monitor out of utter fear. I was going into the forest during the day, finding evidence of Bigfoot, and then staying up at night being frightened by every strange sound and shadow. Often, Dean would stay up with me and try to ease my fear, but nothing really helped. Just the thought of a Bigfoot nearby made me cringe. After countless nights of torment and falling asleep only when completely exhausted, one day I decided to once again face my fear.

I asked Dean to point the cameras with microphones toward the forest, and I increased the volume to intentionally hear them. I wanted to know the moment the Bigfoots arrived, and I was curious to see them. I am reminded of the old saying, "Be careful what you wish for." I figured that once I could establish the normal sounds of our neighborhood, I would then be able to distinguish the sounds of the Bigfoots.

On November 3, after listening to some bizarre sounds, we purchased a handheld recording device and placed it next to the monitor's speaker in the office. This was how we began to record sounds to document the Bigfoots. Remember that I am not an expert and our equipment was not optimal, but it did what we needed it to do, which was record sound so that we could listen to it at the same time. Unfortunately, the dogs could also hear the monitor and sometimes would bark during the recordings, causing them to be heard loud and clear since the device also recorded loud sounds in the office. I mostly recorded sounds from the camera with the microphone mounted on the porch next to our front door. Also because the volume was increased on the monitor, we had static in the recordings. I usually recorded after 8:00 p.m., when the neighborhood was calm and our neighbors were done walking their dogs or jogging by the house. I firmly believed that if you did something long enough, such as listen and watch, you could learn what was normal and what was not. Yes, "Practice makes perfect." When I started this endeavor, I never realized how many sounds were in a neighborhood at night as well as how many animals were in the forest.

We heard a variety of animal sounds, such as those from birds, raccoons, squirrels, owls, and coyotes. In addition, the neighborhood was full of sounds such as cars, trucks, trains, horns, alarms, and a range of other noises that were easily dismissed. However, in our neighborhood, there were sounds that could not be easily explained.

It was 11:55 p.m. when we recorded the monotone cry of a child deep in the forest (Crying#1). We heard this crying once before and louder, but we were not recording at the time. Dean, Jack, and I heard it as we left the office, and it stopped us cold. We stood quietly in the hallway and listened for more in disbelief. It was very late at night, and complete silence followed. It was very strange because we knew there was no child in the forest. Although disturbing to listen to, I was not overly shocked to hear it again, and this time we recorded it. Another disturbing recording, high on the creepy list, was that of a childlike voice calling for its "Mommy" (Mimic #1). It is chilling because no child was outside at 10:33 p.m. looking for its mother. Just listening to this voice sends a chill up your spine because the tone is abnormal. At this point I didn't know what to think of these recordings; however, Mr. Hill did say that Bigfoots liked to mimic children's voices as well as other animals.

One night I purposely recorded our dog Foxy as she did her warning bark, and that recording was beyond bizarre. It had strange sounds of a heartbeat, metal blades, jungle tones, sniffing, and puffing along with other noises that I can't even began to explain. When I listened to that recording, I was horrified and thought, "What the heck is going on in this neighborhood?" I also felt sorry for Foxy. I couldn't believe that was what she had been hearing all these years at night, being tormented by these creatures and repeatedly trying to warn us (Foxy's Warning). Like most dog owners, we were concerned only with her barking late at night and disturbing the neighbors. We never really thought about what she was barking at in her attempts to protect us. Now knowing the importance of her barking, I decided to listen to the other dogs in the neighborhood who also barked aggressively late at night. I suspected Foxy wasn't the only one warning of the beasts.

I noticed Mr. Drake's dogs were sometime left out at night. His backyard, although fenced, was surrounded by the forest. On certain nights they would bark aggressively, out of control, followed by the sounds of snapping branches and leaves being crunched. They were warning us of something traveling through the forest behind his house. Next to Steve and Becky's house, there was a small dog that barked in a panicked tone in the distance. He belonged to a family whose house was on the forest side of the street. Those houses behind Steve and Becky's backyards backed up to the forest. When I heard this little dog, I knew something was traveling through the forest behind those houses. I called these the "dog alarms" because they let me know from which direction something was traveling. It didn't necessarily mean that it was a Bigfoot, because there were other animals in the forest; it just told me that something large was headed our way.

During the night I would also hear other strange sounds and I recorded them as well. One of the most perplexing was that of someone working in the forest after it rained. It sounded like digging, banging, and rocks breaking. It happened a few minutes at a time, sometimes all night long, so it could be very annoying to listen to. As it stopped and started again, I wondered what was being built in the forest during the night and by whom. Also there were strange metal tones in the recordings, and I didn't know what to make of them (Working #1)

I also heard different types of whistles late at night. One was a loud, rapid whistling when the dogs went outside or somebody in the house came home or left. I called it the "warning whistle" because of the strange pattern. There were also other strange bird whistles in the middle of the night as well as loud whistling tunes. They were strange, because at that time of night, it didn't seem normal (Loud Whistle, Bird Whistles).

Strangely, we were also recording sounds close to the microphone on the front porch. I recorded a sniffing and rattling sound (Sniffing #1, Rattling #1). It could just have been a harmless animal milling around in the front yard at night, but I didn't see any. However, our cameras did have blind spots in the front of the house and I didn't know all the animal sounds, so anything was possible.

A clicking noise was also prevalent; it sounded like someone snapping his or her fingers or flicking his or her tongue loudly up against the top of his or her mouth (Clicking). This was one of the sounds I heard the most, in addition to a tapping sound. The tapping sounded like little pebbles hitting the house or two rocks being purposely hit together. Both sounds were infrequent but could occur off and on for hours; this was what made them very odd.

By far, one of the loudest and most horrific sounds coming from the forest was what I believe to be a raccoon screaming followed by an abrupt silence. I found this strange because if two raccoons were fighting, you would hear them and the screams would taper off. It wouldn't be just one horrific scream followed by complete silence (Scream #1).

In addition to learning and recording sounds, I remembered we had a night vision scope and binoculars in the garage with Dean's old military gear. I retrieved them and began learning how to use the equipment. After trying all the windows in the house that faced the forest, I determined our bedroom window on the second floor had the best overall view of the woods. My biggest challenge at night was sneaking in the bedroom while Dean was asleep and quietly scoping the forest. At first, the pups thought it was playtime, so they would jump on me for sneaking in the room and then wake up Dean. Eventually, they learned to ignore me, raising only their heads to watch what I was doing. Some nights they would stay up or sleep downstairs on the couches. They probably got tired of me waking them. The pups were very unpredictable, although I did go to bed in the wee hours of the morning, usually after 3:00 a.m. when I was exhausted.

After learning how to sight the scope, I also had to learn what the forest looked like at night, such as the position of the trees and path. I spent many nights going up and down the stairs while watching and sighting in on certain points in the woods. Some nights the scope was clearer, depending on the amount of moonlight; the scope worked better in complete darkness. Still it was going to be difficult to find the Bigfoots in the forest, since the scope could view only a small section at a time and the forest front was about a quarter of a mile long—not to mention very deep. I didn't know where to start looking; it was similar to finding a needle in a haystack. Also, the scope viewed only in shades of green, from dark to light, and I didn't know what shades of color to focus on. I tried to watch for movement, but if the wind blew, movement was everywhere. I was not an experienced hunter, and it seemed overwhelming, but I was determined to see them. I would learn the forest at night no matter how long it took and eventually find the Bigfoots.

My greatest fear was them seeing me peering through the window at night. I always made sure the room was completely dark before sliding the curtain aside just enough to stick the lens of the scope through. I knew Bigfoots could see in the dark, and I didn't wish to be discovered. However, I believed it was just a matter of time before one of us saw the other.

Staying up all night, listening to sounds, and scoping for Bigfoots were all very tiring, so after several weeks of checking bait and photographing evidence, early in the morning I told Jack it was time to stop. It seemed pointless to continue since we already had enough evidence to show definite proof of the Bigfoots.

6

Provoked

Broken branches

It was a great relief to no longer have to go into the forest, check the bait and photograph it. I could now monitor it from the safety of our home, by recording sound and using the binoculars or night vision scope. I had begun photographing the front of the forest first thing in the morning from the office windows because I noticed something odd was occurring. Strangely, to the right of the entrance path, some of the trees along the front were being peeled overnight and the limbs were being broken. The way the limbs were broken was what looked suspicious to me, above the five-foot level, forming large holes between the trees like observation points. In addition, something had been forming strange pathways from the back of the forest to the front. I could see down them as I looked out the window.

One morning, I opened up the office shades again to take pictures and snapped a few when something between the trees moved. This wasn't overly alarming because sometimes the squirrels jumped from tree to tree, causing this type of movement. I continued to photograph the area when suddenly a large maple tree in the front of the forest shook violently. Its leaves were a brilliant orange, and the trees around it were Evergreens, so I clearly saw it shake from top to bottom all at once. In disbelief, I froze, momentarily staring at the forest as a cold chill went down my spine. An eerie sense of being watched came over me as I stood at the window; it felt as if something was sending me a message. In an attempt to see what shook the tree, I grabbed the binoculars, but the forest was too thick. After I watched for a while, eventually, I gave up.

As the day went by, I concentrated on other things, such as another creepy recording of the childlike voice. This strange voice was calling out again for its "Mommy." We recorded it at 10:15 p.m., and it sounded disturbingly close to our house (Mimic #2). I had mentioned to Mr. Hill this childlike voice as well as the crying coming from the forest, and he said it was probably a male Bigfoot mimicking a child. He had several cases where people reported hearing children's voices and crying in the middle of a forest. Either way, these recordings were concerning.

On the morning of November 18, I was taking pictures from the office window again when I saw a dark image moving in the forest. This time, I immediately grabbed the binoculars to see what it was, but the forest was still too dense. I searched and searched, believing it was a Bigfoot hiding in the trees, and I could feel its eyes staring at me. Seeing nothing unusual in the forest, I realized how ridiculous it was to feel this way—I couldn't be afraid every time something moved across the street, especially in broad daylight. My logical reasoning worked for a bit, yet I couldn't shake the feeling of being watched. While sitting at the desk with my back to the window, I kept looking over my shoulder. Unable to concentrate, I stood up and stared at the forest again. Wishing I could see deeper into the woods, I studied the forest very carefully and noticed it was the lower branches on the trees that were blocking my view. If we cut them, a Bigfoot wouldn't be able to stand there without being seen.

When Dean awoke that morning, I told him what had happened and explained my idea. Since he already mowed and maintained the easement across the street, he quickly agreed because, evidently, the lower branches were scratching him as he mowed underneath them. He figured it was a win-win situation since I agreed to help. That afternoon we spent most of the day trimming at least fifty feet to the right of the forest entrance. This part was in my line of sight from the office window. When we were finished, we could see at least thirty feet into the forest. It was a long day—and we figured it would also be a long night. The Bigfoots would not be happy, and we anticipated some type of response.

Exhausted, we came back inside, and I fell asleep. By the time I awoke, the night was nearly over. Upset that I probably missed recording the Bigfoots, I rushed downstairs to turn on the monitor. When I got to the office, the light was on, and there was Dean sitting at the desk and listening to the forest. He had stayed awake to monitor it because he felt I needed the sleep.

I asked him whether anything had happened and he said, "Yes, something strange did happen. Around 10:20 p.m. I heard loud voices that sounded like a man and a woman arguing. It was so loud that I went outside to see who was yelling. I went to the middle of the street and looked around, but it was dead quiet, so I came back inside and it has been quiet since." I asked whether he had set the recording device. He said he had—it was on the whole time. I was very pleased that I hadn't missed anything. Exhausted, Dean was finally able to get some sleep.

After Dean went to bed, I pulled the recording device to hear the yelling. I couldn't believe what I was hearing. It was bizarre and foreign. I listened to it a few times and tried to make sense of the words. It was some type of language that reminded me of an ancient dialect spoken in a weird tongue, and the main voice was very deep and penetrating, similar to the howl we had heard before. It had to be a Bigfoot (Language #1).

The next morning I contacted Mr. Hill and e-mailed him a copy of the recording to analyze. He listened to it and said he would try to remove some of the static and would call us back. When he did later that afternoon, he confirmed my suspicion.

"It sure sounds like the Bigfoots," he said. "The language is consistent in how they form speech, with the lack of vowels."

I was thrilled to know that we had recorded them speaking in their language, because I had no idea they even had a language of their own; I thought they just made animal sounds and mimicked voices. I thanked Mr. Hill and asked how he removed the static, and he mentioned a computer program he used. It sounded like just what we needed, so I downloaded it and began using it to clean up our recordings as best I could.

To me, the yelling meant progress. They obviously were not happy with us clearing that large section of forest and disrupting their ability to hide. We now had an unobstructed view during the day, so if they were awake they couldn't watch us. Also maybe the car lights at night would penetrate deeper into the forest and disrupt them. I was trying purposely to discourage the Bigfoots from coming to this part of the forest. Finally, we had the upper hand, and maybe they would leave.

The next night started out calm and quiet, with no indications of a Bigfoot nearby. Dean and I were talking in the office. Although we were listening to the sounds of the forest, we had the monitor volume on low. We really didn't think anything was going to happen. Foxy wanted to go out, and it was 10:30

p.m. We decided to let her outside only because we didn't think she would bark. Of course, we were wrong—the minute she went outside, she began her warning bark, and something very strange happened.

I quickly turned up the volume on the monitor to hear what was happening. This ended up being one of our worst recordings because I kept switching the microphones back and forth. Unfortunately, the cameras with microphones were on the same monitor, and you could listen to only one at a time. The camera over the garage picked up the sound to the left of the forest, while the camera over the front door covered the area more to the right. I also kept increasing the volume since some of the events took place more than a block away. Even though this was not one of our best recordings, I did learn not to switch the microphones or increase the volume during one.

However, when listening to this occurrence live, we came to the conclusion that someone was chasing a Bigfoot. I labeled this recording "The Chase." On the tape, you first hear Foxy barking, and a few seconds later, you hear the beeping sound of commercial vehicles backing up. A minute later, you hear what we saw on the monitor—two white vans with only driver's-side windows speeding by the house. A helicopter was also going over the house and hovering above in the distance. With my attempt to clean up the tape, I might have removed some of the sounds (Chase part 1). In our final version of the recording, in the background, you could hear something large moving quickly through the forest, snapping branches. Also in the distance was the sound of a man's voice yelling something? (Chase part 2).

This part of the recording was difficult to hear because it was happening a block away, but I amplified the man's voice yelling (Chase Voice). Remember that this all was taking place between 10:30 and 10:40 p.m. Finally, there are loud banging sounds followed by more sounds of movement in the forest. At the end, all became silent, and the rest of the night was peaceful.

The next day I called Mr. Hill and told him what happened. He said he would stop by the next day to hear the recording. I felt like a huge burden had been lifted because I assumed the Bigfoots had been removed the night before.

Though I had no idea who performed the task, I really didn't care; I was just thrilled they were gone. The monitor was still on as I sat in the office, and I began to hear footsteps of a four-legged animals walking through the forest. Quickly opening up the blinds, I grabbed the binoculars to see what it was. To my delight, I saw three deer heading toward Mr. Drake's house, probably going to the park across from him. I was thrilled because I could clearly see them in the forest due to our trimming.

As day turned to night, all was peaceful and quiet. I peeked out a few times with the night vision scope and saw nothing, as usual. There was some movement in the forest but nothing loud or crashing. Believing they were gone, I turned off the monitor and slept very peacefully that night for the first time in a long while.

7

Nightmare Incarnate

Weaving of forest

On the morning of November 21, I opened the shades in the office, excited to hopefully see deer moving through the forest again. Believing that the Bigfoots were gone, I saw the forest in a different light and wanted to enjoy the wildlife in it. It was a beautiful morning after a good night's sleep. I grabbed the binoculars and pointed them at the forest while looking between the trees when suddenly I realized something was terribly wrong. I could barely see past the first set of trees. Somehow the forest had grown thicker overnight. How was this possible? Yesterday, I could clearly see at least thirty feet into the forest, but today I could barely see five feet.

Bewildered, I ran upstairs and woke up Dean to tell him something was happening in the forest. He threw on his cowboy boots and Levi's and packed his pistol. I grabbed my coat and camera, and we headed into the forest to investigate. As we cautiously entered the wooded area, we immediately saw the cause of the change. The vines appeared twisted around the trees forming strange shapes. The saplings, low branches, and hanging vines were being woven together, catching the nettles and leaves as they fell from the trees. It reminded me of military camouflage netting, the kind Dean would bring home for the boys to play with. Some of the vines and saplings were shaped into elaborate arches like the kind that you would stand under to enter a garden. It was the most amazing thing, and the architecture of these arches was impressive. Farther in the forest, the ground once covered in leaves yet clear to walk through looked like a maze of raised vines with walking paths behind them. There were mounds of leaves and piles of stacked branches. Dean noticed that the limbs he cut were moved and restacked farther back in the forest. He said he knew for sure he didn't put them there.

The Bigfoots appeared to be in the process of building a new forest thicket to hide behind. Dean found what appeared to be a Bigfoot warning sign at the bottom of a large tree. It too was not there three days before when we cut back the forest. I had a terrible feeling after seeing the amount of work involved in reshaping the forest—no two Bigfoots could have done this overnight. Dean and I agreed, took pictures, and left.

100 Bigfoot Nights

Late that afternoon, Mr. Hill stopped by to hear "The Chase" recording. After listening to it, he said on the tape it did sound like someone was chasing a Bigfoot, but he didn't know who. I asked whether he thought they had caught it.

"No, they didn't catch it," he replied. "There is no way to contain one with a van. They would need a special facility to contain a live one. They would have to kill it, and if they had shot it, even with a tranquilizing gun, it would have been hollering and screaming on your tape. I have interviewed hunters when they shot one, and believe me, the whole neighborhood would know if it was shot. They are incredibly loud."

I had a horrible feeling in the pit of my stomach as I sat there and listened to him. His words were not comforting to me, but I suspected after looking at the forest that the Bigfoots were not gone. Something told me this was only the beginning and I was in for more sleepless nights. This nightly torment was going to continue despite my wanting it to end. Mr. Hill had to go, but he was curious as to who would have chased the Bigfoots. I, on the other hand, hoped they would return to finish the job.

Later that evening, Jack and I were talking in the office when we heard a horrible scream. It sounded like a raccoon being killed—chilling screams followed by sudden silence. Although disturbing, it was not too unusual since I had heard it twice before. I suspected the Bigfoots sometimes killed the raccoons and there was nothing we could do about it. Soon after the scream we heard a faint growl followed by branches snapping and voices coming from the forest.

We quickly switched to the monitor over the garage and saw flashlights near the forest entrance. It was our next-door neighbors, Mike and Carla, with their eighteen-year-old daughter, Sara, standing in the street. I figured something must have happened, so I went outside to speak with them. As I exited the house, Carla and Sara met me on my driveway. They had shocked looks on their faces—Carla's hazel eyes were wide open, and her demeanor was unsettled. She was shaking with her arms crossed and not dressed properly for the cold. Sara was also shaking, and her big blue eyes were intense as she timidly held her hands over her mouth. I saw Mike in the forest with a flashlight, searching for something, so I asked what happened.

Carla said, "You won't believe what just happened to us." She told me Sara was outside saying good-bye to her boyfriend on their driveway when she heard a horrible scream coming from the forest. It frightened her so much that she went inside to get them.

"We grabbed our flashlights and ran out the door," she recounted. "I didn't even have time to grab my coat. We got about ten feet from the forest path when we heard the most frightening growl, and then something large slid down a tree. We could hear the branches snapping and a loud thump as it landed on the ground. It sounded big. I swear the ground shook when it landed."

Sara spoke up and said, "I heard it too because I was right behind them."

"We heard loud footsteps moving in two different directions," Carla continued. "It startled us so much we stopped and looked at each other. I said to Mike, 'What was that?' I think my heart skipped a beat."

"It frightened me too," said Sara. She was still shaking and stared into the forest as she tried to keep an eye on her dad.

Carla reemphasized as she too watched the forest. "We just couldn't believe the sound," she said. "I think we startled something big." She nervously laughed and added, "Mike mentioned that you think there's Bigfoots in the forest?"

"Yes," I replied, "and I think you startled them. I've heard them growl before, so I know how scary it can be, although I never had one jump out of a tree. That must be terrifying."

She shook her head yes as she kept her eyes on the forest. I began to tell Carla about the investigation. She explained that she had seen Mr. Hill in the forest and Mike had even spoken with him on several occasions, so she was aware of it.

"This is crazy!" she said. "I can't believe this is happening. I get the chills every time I think about it. You know I walk Jake [their dog] by the forest every night. We usually go toward the corner to Mr. Drake's house because he likes to visit with their dogs. There were many times I would hear something following me in the forest. At first I thought it was a bear, but it would stop when I stopped and walked when I walked. It would make me so nervous that I wouldn't allow Jake near the forest and we'd stay in the street or on your side of it. I can't even begin to tell you all the strange noises I would hear. I told Mike many times that I swore something was in there following me."

"I know what you mean," I said. "I always felt something was in the forest too, but I never imagined it was a Bigfoot."

I began to tell her more about the evidence we had collected when all of a sudden we heard something loud hit the street by Mr. Drake's house. Mike was near it and came out of the forest. He yelled over to us, asking whether we had heard the noise. He said something was thrown at him and it landed in the street. By this time, Dean and Jack had come outside with flashlights and also heard Mike yelling from the corner. We told them what happened, so they went to search the forest by Mr. Drake's house.

With all the men in the forest chasing Bigfoots, we were going to be outside for a while, so Carla and Sara went home to get their coats. I decided to call Mr. Hill to let him know what was happening. He said he would be right there. I went back outside and stood on the front porch in the dark, alone, waiting for him to arrive or someone to return. Then, all of a sudden, I smelled a putrid odor. It was radiating from all directions and encompassing me. The stench was so strong I felt ill. Not knowing where it was coming from, I immediately ran in the house and locked the door. Ten minutes later, Mr. Hill arrived, and I went outside to greet him and noticed the smell was somehow gone. Carla and Sara also returned, and they too met us on my driveway. A few seconds later, Mike emerged from the forest, but still there was no sign of Dean or Jack.

Mike, Carla, and Sara began to tell Mr. Hill what happened and pointed out where they were standing when they heard the frightening sounds. Mike and Mr. Hill went back into the forest with flashlights and retraced his steps. In the meantime, Dean and Jack returned and decided to go through the forest in a different direction. They wanted to check the left side of it behind Steve and Becky's house. Once again Carla, Sara, and I stood in the driveway in front of my house and waited for them to return. I was not going into the forest, and neither were they. They were still shocked and in disbelief, while I was thinking how dangerous this was becoming.

Mike and Mr. Hill searched the street to find what was thrown at Mike. They found a medium-size river rock about the size of a man's palm. They suspected the rock was thrown near him as a warning to stay away. Maybe he was getting too close while pursuing them. Mr. Hill gave Mike the rock as a souvenir for the night he chased the Bigfoots.

After the excitement died down, and with Dean and Jack back safely, we said goodnight to our neighbors, and we all went home. Mr. Hill stayed for a few minutes while Dean made a fresh pot of coffee to warm everyone. We were discussing the evening events when Jack mentioned that, while in the forest, he heard footsteps following him. They had been to the right, somewhere in the bushes. He told us that every time he took a step, he heard a step, and when he stopped, it stopped. He said it was as if it was echoing his footsteps. Mr. Hill explained that this was common Bigfoot behavior. They watched you and mirrored your movement; they walked when you walked and kept a good eye on you.

"It felt like I was being watched," Jack said. "It happened when my dad and I were separated and I went farther back into the forest by the creek."

Jack was surprised that he couldn't see the Bigfoot hiding in the bushes. It was getting late, so Mr. Hill had to go. We thanked him for coming so quickly. He was very pleased to get an incident report directly from the neighbors' right after the event.

Later that night, I was sitting in the office and again listening to the sounds of the forest. All was quiet, and I figured the Bigfoots would be gone for at least a few days after being chased. So you could imagine my surprise when I heard the sound of them and knew they were back. I could hardly believe my ears. Any animal would have stayed away, but obviously, they were not like other animals. Why did they return so soon?

Thanks to our neighbors, I now had a clue as to their whereabouts in the forest. It was a cluster of trees and low brush to the left of the forest entrance. If I was ever going to see the Bigfoots, now was my chance. Without thinking twice, I grabbed the night vision scope and headed upstairs to our bedroom. I was determined to find them.

At 10:45 p.m., Dean tried to go to bed, but I was not giving up spying out our bedroom window. The pups were jumping around a lot, so he decided to take them and go sleep in the spare bedroom. He said if I needed him I should just wake him up. Although Dean was struggling to understand my obsessive fear of the Bigfoots, he was still very supportive of my wanting to see them. He attempted a few times to use the night vision scope, but due to vision changes, it caused his vertigo to kick in. Besides, he would rather hunt them through the forest than see them standing in it.

After what seemed to be a long time, finally something moved between the trees, and the color changed. It was about eight feet up in the middle of them. Some of the branches were missing or pushed aside. I saw a dark hole, and something was peeking through it. It looked like a large head and kept appearing and disappearing inside the hole, slowly swaying from side to side. I watched to make sure it wasn't an owl because it appeared to have large, round eyes. When it leaned out a little farther, I caught a glimpse of a complete face and neck attached to a shoulder, and it was no owl. My blood ran cold and my heart was racing. I couldn't believe he was right there, hiding in the thicket along the forest front. If you would have walked along the easement, he could have bitten you—that's how close he was. I watched as a car drove by, and he didn't flinch. He just leaned back into the darkness and disappeared.

I continued to watch the cluster of trees when suddenly there was another movement along the side of them. It was another Bigfoot that was lowing himself down from behind the tall patch of trees. He was trying to hide behind a shallow thicket next to them in order to move along the front of the forest without being seen. It looked as if he was low, crawling behind it, because his back was swaying back and forth as he moved along

Christine D. Parker

55

the forest bottom. I could see him behind the thicket because of my elevated position, but I couldn't see his bottom half, so he could have been down on all fours, but his back didn't appear sloped. I estimated the shallow thicket was about three and a half feet tall. As I watched him slowly crawling, I couldn't believe how wide his back was—it was huge. He stayed low behind the thicket until he reached another set of trees further back in the forest. At first I thought I lost him as he went behind the trees, but I quickly realized that I wasn't viewing a large bush along the side of the trees—it was moving! He had stood up.

I was shocked because he was so large with rough edges of hair that I assumed he was a bush. Never had I seen something that large moving through a forest. Frozen with fear, I nearly passed out from holding my breath. Surely, I thought they would discover me peeking through the window, so I backed away and sat down at the edge of the bed. I felt physically ill and struggled to breathe. My heart was pounding out of control, and my mind was racing. I touched my face, and it hurt from being distorted as I watched. I had a horrible feeling after watching something I was not supposed to see just outside our bedroom window.

I took a break closed my eyes and waited to calm down, before forcing myself watch them again, this time wanting to see their faces. As I searched the forest again, further to the left, I was completely stunned because there were so many. I struggled to comprehend what I was seeing, it was too overwhelming and I nearly blacked out and hit the floor. Trying to regain my composure I quickly refocused the scope to only watch a small one sitting in a tree. He was moving his head back and forth, shaking the tree with his mouth wide open, as if he was yelling from the treetops. I was able to see a side profile of him. He had a thick upper brow that made his eyes seem recessed and the face of an animal—like a gorilla but with a pointed nose at the end of his snout.

The chilling sense of not knowing what we were dealing with came over me. Terrified and traumatized, I quickly backed away from the window and sat on the bed again rubbing my aching stomach in disbelief. What the hell were those hideous creatures in the forest? Was this what a Bigfoot looked like?

Horrified, sick and frightened, I buried myself under the covers on the bed and eventually fell asleep.

8

Beastly Faces

Moving beasts

The next day I told Dean I had seen the Bigfoots in the forest and described to him the terror I felt while watching them. Still in shock, I felt lost and confused by what I had seen. For so many reasons, Mr. Hill said there were only two, yet I had seen a large group of them. We assumed these elusive creatures were rare, and there weren't that many. How could we be so wrong? He also said they had human looking faces and that too was not the case. Although I did only see the side profile of the smaller one and couldn't be sure they all had beastly faces. The only thing I felt for sure was they were not here to run from anyone. There was no way they could have. Although they were quiet and moved cautiously, through the forest they engulfed the left side of it near Steve and Becky's house. Based on their behavior and the lack of fear, I concluded that they had returned with reinforcements to retake their territory. This was the only thing that made sense, because growing up in California I knew this was common gang behavior. Run off two and they return with ten.

It was Thanksgiving Day, November 22; I was so distracted replaying the images from the night before that it ruined the holiday. Throughout the day, I talked to Dean about them. I wanted to know what he thought. To me, the world had changed overnight, and it was a new world that made no sense. I was desperate for any logical answers. Because it was the holiday, I didn't call Mr. Hill; we knew he had family visiting, and after only seeing them one horrific time I couldn't be absolutely sure of the beastly faces. Dean was very good at calming me, but he too had some questions that we couldn't answer. In order to verify their faces I need to see them again, even though I was afraid too.

Later that evening, I was once again monitoring the forest and waiting for them. The motion sensor lights activated a few times, but it was nothing unusual. I watched the monitor for any additional shadows on the front porch because I sensed something was nearby.

At 9:35 p.m., I heard the aggressive barking of Mr. Drake's dogs followed by the sounds of branches snapping and leaves crunching in the forest. I knew the Bigfoots were there, so I grabbed the night vision scope and went upstairs to watch them again. Dean was awake and watching television in the family room, so I was less apprehensive about seeing them. I quickly told Dean what was happening, and he asked whether I needed him.

Knowing that the pups would follow, I replied, "No, it's OK. I can do this."

As I reached our bedroom, I stopped to take a few calming breaths. I turned off the hallway light so none of it reflected into the dark bedroom. I cautiously entered the room careful not to make any noise for fear that somehow they would hear. Sneaking in the room was a familiar pattern since I had done it many times before. Slowly and carefully, I placed the scope through the curtains and began searching for them. Amazingly, now that I knew what shade of color to look for compared to the surrounding forest, I was quickly able to spot them.

I counted three of them along the sides of the path. One was hiding on the left side of a bush, behind some branches by the forest edge. He was moving the branches slowly and cautiously every now and then so he could observe the street. I could see only the image of him and the top of his head; he never exposed his whole face. He appeared stocky looking with broad shoulders. I didn't think he was standing because he wasn't very tall.

On the opposite side of the path under a berry bush was another one. I could see a silhouette of its body underneath the bush. It was a wide, dark figure crouching and forming an odd shape. It was also slightly moving under the bush and doing something with its arms.

Farther down the path next to the one under the bush, there was one more active. He was standing upright yet not straight, rapidly moving his long arms and doing something to the branches above his head. He seemed to be moving his arms very fast, which caused the darkness to spin. It was very strange because there were also flashes of light and I got the impression he was creating them.

Christine D. Parker

I scoped for the others, and they were in the trees. Between them I could see movement. Again there were many in the forest. They seemed to range in size because I also saw movement close to the ground. Some were the shade of the Bigfoots, but some were not. After seeing these light-colored apparitions, I felt physically ill and figured my eyes were definitely strained.

I went back downstairs and sat quietly in the office. I had a dreaded feeling that we were in danger. My neck and back were tense, and I sensed a heavy weight on my shoulders. Who's going to believe what is happening around here? I wondered. I felt like I was in the *Twilight Zone*—a television show about bizarre things that happen to ordinary people—because this was truly bizarre: elusive creatures hiding in plain sight in a neighborhood, knowing we can't see two feet in a forest at night. Mr. Hill was right when he said they were intelligent. They somehow knew how to stay hidden and avoid the enticements of urbanization.

A while later, Dean was looking for me, but he didn't know I was downstairs in the office. He was headed upstairs when he noticed me with a concerned look on my face, so he asked whether I had seen the Bigfoots again. I told him yes, along with other things, and it was not good. He could tell I was extremely stressed, so he hugged me and made my favorite snack. We talked about the situation, and he tried to comfort me.

He said, "According to Mr. Hill, they have been here for years and haven't hurt anyone, so you need not be so afraid."

But I was afraid—very afraid—and I couldn't understand why Dean and our sons didn't feel the same way. However, I knew what they looked like, and I was terrified.

"I go outside all the time at night," he said, "and I haven't seen them so obviously they hide."

It was common for Dean to go out in the evening, to get fast food, check the mail, gas the vehicles or rearrange them in the driveway. So I knew what he meant. The Bigfoots were probably use to seeing him outside and didn't view him as a threat. Not to mention he always made a lot of noise, Dean wasn't very quiet. The Bigfoots could easily hear him, so they chose to hide.

By the time we finished talking I felt a little better, it was late so Dean and I went to bed; however, I took the scope and watched the creatures a few more times throughout the night, and again what I saw was disturbing.

Exhausted, I slept most of the next day and woke up well after dark. I quickly went into the office to turn on the monitor and set the recording device. As the hours passed, I noticed lots of activity outside; the motion sensor lights kept switching from high to low. I had the strange feeling that the Bigfoots were testing the lights. I heard subtle sounds of branches breaking every once in a while and constant tapping as little pebbles hit the house. I had already learned the sounds and knew once again they were here. It took a few minutes to ready myself to see them again.

It was 10:15 p.m. Dean and William were talking in the kitchen. As I headed up the stairs, I felt anxious since once again the unknown awaited me. I took a calming breathe and then focused the scope on the forest path. The three Bigfoots were there again in similar positions as the night before, except the one under the berry bush was at the edge of it, squatting down and eating something. It looked like a female because it was smaller and less muscular than the others I had seen. She had longer hair around her face, large hands, and a protruding mouth. She was rubbing her mouth using both hands at the same time, and her arms were much longer in proportion to the rest of her body. There was also a dark shape moving next to her on the ground. It looked like a toddler with a seamless hair outfit moving awkwardly along the edge of the forest path. It was hard to make out any detail because it was small and low; it could have been another animal. I was focusing on the little critter when a larger one standing behind the thicket suddenly emerged. I hadn't realized he was there. He was about the size of a man, muscular but thin. I caught a glimpse of him from the side; he was wiggling his snout and sniffing the night air. He seemed alert as he tilted his upper body and head upward. Perhaps it was my imagination, but I suspected that he sensed I was watching him because he boldly emerged. It scared me half to death, so I quickly stopped and stealthily left the room.

The rest of the night I heard strange sounds close to the microphone on the front porch. I wish I knew why they sounded so close. It always concerned me, especially when the motion sensor lights kept activating throughout the entire front of the house. Sometimes the frequency of the microphone changed like the music in a horror picture when you know something bad is about to happen. Our nightly recordings were full of subtle sounds of something sneaking around at night, so this was nothing new. At 2:30 in the morning, Dean came into the office. We talked for a while and then went to bed. However, after listening to the audio recording from that night, something was calling from the forest a 3:35 a.m., and it sounded like it was expecting a response (Three Calls).

After watching the beasts repeatedly for a few days and seeing the most bizarre things, I finally told our sons, especially Jack, that the Bigfoots I had been watching were not the ones Mr. Hill had described. What I was watching appeared to be something different. I was apprehensive about saying anything because I didn't want to seem foolish. But I was now sure some had animal-like faces and I didn't want Jack outside anymore shooting a flashlight into the forest.

I called Mr. Hill to tell him what I had observed and gave the best description I could.

He asked a few questions and said, "OK, I think I know what you are referring to. The kind you are describing is a *type* of Bigfoot. There are different kinds of Bigfoots. One is more animal-like than the other. It sounds like you have what I call a *Type 2*. They're more aggressive because they are more animal-like. There will be a news report shortly," he added, "but it will be referring to the large, human-looking, reddish-brown-haired ones."

I was curious, but he couldn't tell us more. He just stated that it would make the news. He had to go but said he would stop by later and inform us about this type of Bigfoot. I was completely shocked by what he said—we didn't know there were different types of Bigfoots! This revelation was frightening at first, and I was very upset. But after talking to Dean, we realized it really made no difference what type was in the forest. Our situation was the same regardless, and we already suspected they were aggressive and dangerous.

Later that evening, Dean and I were sitting in the office while monitoring the forest when Jack came in and asked to use the computer. He told us that he had seen news about a team of scientists who had been studying the DNA of Bigfoot for the past five years. We read the report, and it was big news in the Bigfoot world. It proved that they existed.

"I wish a team of scientists could come to our house and capture these Bigfoots," I said to Jack.

I felt like sending an e-mail to this scientific team and saying, "Hello, could you please come to our house and map out this other species? And, by the way, feel free to remove them. You can even stay at our house as long as you like—just catch these things." Our situation seemed overwhelming, but I figured the scientists would find out eventually. Now that Mr. Hill was aware of the *type* of Bigfoot.

For the past few weeks I had also been chasing shadows in the forest during the day. Some of them were suspicious looking, and I suspected they were more than just shadows. The leaves were beginning to fall, and the forest looked extra dark and creepy. I had been leaving the microphones on during the day, especially after the tree-shaking incident, and we recorded sounds of something large moving through the forest, snapping branches and crunching leaves. The sounds were familiar to our nighttime recordings, except there was a crow calling in a weird pattern and birds chirping in a panicked tone. Something was creating the dark moving shadows and causing a disturbance, and I was trying to find out what it was.

On November 25, after countless times of going up and down the stairs with binoculars, I finally saw what was causing the disturbance. It was a Bigfoot. I could hardly believe my eyes when I caught him standing in broad daylight behind the thicket between some trees. It was one thing to see them at night through a night vision scope—they were colorless and fuzzy looking. But this one was clear, in full color, and I literally could see him breathe.

He was standing to the left of the forest entrance about ten feet back. Through the binoculars I could clearly see his upper torso, arms, and hands. He was standing upright and scratching the inside of his arm using the back of his other hand, rubbing continuously from the forearm to the inside of his elbow. His long arms were slightly bent as he scratched very slowly with the back of his hand using his fingertips. My mind was overwhelmed by the sight of him, and for some reason, I kept counting his fingers repeatedly. There were five digits per hand. He had dark black hair and a medium-length, even, full coat, except that on his arms near the shoulders, his hair was a little longer, with silver on the tips. I assumed it was male because he didn't have large protruding breasts and his arms were muscular. His chest had less hair and was lighter in color. He was facing toward the street and our home. I couldn't see his head because branches were in the way.

I mentally marked his position using bushes and trees and then feverishly ran around the house to the other windows, in a desperate attempt to see his face. The branches obstructed my view of him from every window downstairs. Disappointed, I ran back upstairs to watch him again through my bedroom window. He was still there next to Steve and Becky's house. I didn't know what to do. I was frantic seeing this beast watching our house in broad daylight.

I wanted to take a picture, but I couldn't. My camera wouldn't focus at that distance. The pups had eaten our good camera a month prior, and I would be getting a new one for Christmas, but that was a month away. Everyone in the house was gone except Adam; he was in his bedroom still asleep. I yelled for him to come quickly to see the Bigfoot.

Hearing me yell, Adam quickly woke up and ran into the room because he thought something was wrong. To his surprise and dismay, I handed him the binoculars and explained to him what was happening. Since he was now awake, he agreed to look through the binoculars. He looked for a few minutes but couldn't see what I was talking about because he couldn't understand my directions. After a few more minutes of my explaining, he did finally find the shadow of the Bigfoot casting across the forest floor. I repeatedly kept telling him to look at the shadow and follow it behind the thicket and between the trees.

"I can see the shadow," he said. "It looks like a head, body, and arm of something. But I can't find the Bigfoot."

It was 10 o'clock in the morning; I couldn't understand why he was having trouble following the shadow. I couldn't give him any clearer directions. Frustrated at me for repeating the directions, he said, "I'll just go just outside and look," as he handed me the binoculars and headed downstairs.

"Fine," I replied, "and when he runs, I will get a better look at him."

I grabbed the binoculars to spot the Bigfoot again, but I couldn't find him or his shadow. Since Adam was already headed downstairs and toward the forest. I figured if the Bigfoot was still nearby, it might move as Adam approached and maybe I would be able to see its face. I watched Adam as he carefully walked across the street toward the forest where he had seen the shadow. He approached very slowly, carefully viewing the forest from the easement. From there he could see at least twenty feet in to the forest without having to go in it. I watched the forest through the binoculars, and nothing moved. Disappointed again I came downstairs and sat at the desk in the office.

When Adam came back inside, he told me, nothing was there. "Not even the shadow?" he said with a bewildered look on his face.

I quickly replied, "I know; after you handed me the binoculars, I looked again, and I couldn't find him. I tried to let you see the Bigfoot and missed getting a good look at him as he left."

He ran back upstairs with the binoculars to verify that the shadow was gone. I guess he thought maybe he was in the wrong place outside; I really didn't care. When he came back downstairs, he sat on the couch in the office with a perplexed look on this face and he shook his head and reiterated how disturbing it was that the shadow was gone.

After Adam left the room, I thought about what had happened. I should have described the Bigfoot to him so he knew what to look for but at the time I was too anxious and upset.

To me, not being able to photograph the Bigfoot and see its face were both huge disappointments. It was bad enough that I watched them night after night with no way to photograph what I was seeing, but now they were there during the day and yet I was still unable to get a photo. Despite my frustration, it was also very unnerving seeing this beast awake during the day, watching our neighborhood, looking relaxed as if he had done this many times before.

9

Frantic

Never thought this would happen to me, but it has, and so it shall be told. I have approahced this as open-minded, skeptical, and thorough as possible. It's a long and detailed story, so bear with me.

There's a forest across my street with pretty thick folliage (with the exception of a small trail) and has a creek passing through it, down in a gully. I've lived in this home for 6-7 years but it wasn't really until the 13th that the story begins.

My dad was outside fiddling with Halloween decorations that he set up earlier....

Excerpt from Jack's online investigation

The following day Mr. Hill stopped by, and I pointed out to him where I had seen the Bigfoots in the forest. I also informed him of the daytime sighting. He listened with concern then suggested that he could place a gaming camera in the forest, along with a recording device and some bait. He was apprehensive about placing the camera because he said sometimes Bigfoots ripped the cameras from the trees and destroyed them, and he didn't like replacing cameras. We understood his dilemma, but we really needed pictures of them. So I was glad that he had decided to do it. He left and retuned a few hours later with a ladder, gaming camera, recording device, and a piece of raw liver. By the time everything was set up, it was dusk, and he came inside to talk with us.

We showed him how we recorded sound and what our cameras viewed at night. When it was time for him to go, he told us that when we heard a branch break, followed by lots of noises, we should just record it. He would be back in the morning to check the camera and bait. With the bait and camera outside, we were expecting some activity. Dean suggested we take turns sleeping on the couch in the office and monitoring the forest. I would take the first shift of monitoring, and he would take the second. This way we could both get some sleep.

The night was surprisingly quiet, with no activity outside at all. Even our motion sensor lights activated only when or sons arrived home. It was getting later, and Dean was calmly sleeping in the office along with all the dogs. At 10:30 p.m., I needed to stretch my legs, so I decided to go upstairs and scope the forest. Even though I heard no signs of them, I figured it wouldn't hurt to check outside. I picked up the night vision scope and quietly left the room, careful not to wake Dean or the dogs. I was expecting to go upstairs, see nothing, and quietly return. Of course, that's not what happened.

I began to check the forest by focusing on the path when I noticed rapid movement in the brush to the left of the entrance. It was a Bigfoot moving his arms rapidly along the side of the path while hiding behind the brush. I was surprised he was there because I didn't hear him arrive. He was acting strangely,

100 Bigfoot Nights

moving his arms in haste so close to the street. I thought he must have found the gaming camera because he seemed irritated. His arms were moving so fast I could see only his body outline, and his behavior was very strange. His rapid arm movement wasn't serving any obvious purpose, so I got the impression he was signaling something—but to whom? I looked across from him and saw some movement but nothing discernible. It just seemed awfully blank.

He had to be communicating with another, I thought, as I tried again to focus down the right side of the path along the trees. I found it very odd that I couldn't see the trees down the path or the reflections of moonlight on the floor. As a matter of fact, I couldn't see anything.

For some reason I was more curious than frightened, although I did have to take a break. Baffled, I lowered the scope to relieve my arm and closed my eyes to rest them for a few minutes. Then I started over scoping the path. I kept adjusting the focus back and forth, trying to pick up an image, but still I couldn't see anything. So I focused on the trees above the path and slowly began to move the scope downward. Something caught my eye—it was a silhouette of a head with the moonlight and forest behind it. I looked down and to the right and saw a body and two separate arms. I looked up and to the right and saw another head. I continued to move the scope and saw two more. There were four large Bigfoots standing shoulder to shoulder at the edge of darkness. They were blocking the path and facing our house. My heart skipped a beat, and I nearly dropped the scope because they were so huge.

I ran downstairs as fast as I could. When I reached the office, I was shaking and out of breath. I quickly woke Dean, and he immediately jumped up and saw the horrified look on my face. The dogs were also startled. They began barking and jumping around. I was extremely upset because I had never seen Bigfoots that large before and they were awfully quiet, staring at our house. They had what appeared to be longer hair and massive-looking bodies. Similar I suppose to the one's Mr. Hill had described. After catching my breath and calming the dogs down, I was finally able to tell Dean about the Bigfoots standing on the path.

After describing them to him I said, "The small one seemed really upset. I don't know where the large ones came from but they are huge, at least ten feet or taller. I think they found the gaming camera and are deciding want to do about it. Do you think they are smart enough to know we had something to do with it?"

"I don't know," Dean replied.

"Well," I said, "if they decide to do something we're in deep trouble because they could easily destroy our house. Their so big nothing would stop them. Remember, when Mr. Hill told us that they have attacked home before by banging on them and throwing large rocks."

"Yeah," Dean said, "and I suspect Mr. Hill hasn't told us everything they do."

"I think putting the camera in the forest was a huge mistake because they were staring at the house. What should we do?" I asked.

Dean said, "Every things going to be OK," in a calming voice, as he opened up the desk drawer and pull out his 357 Magnum. He then opened up his gun cabinet and loaded a few rifles and placed them around the house. He said, "Just in case."

We also turned on all the lights on the bottom floor as well as any extra exterior lighting. Figuring this might detour them. It was terrifying thinking about what could happen. For the first time it dawned on me that maybe irritating the Bigfoots wasn't a good idea.

As the hours passed, we talked about our situation and how insane it was becoming; we couldn't even call for help. Who would believe this was happening in a middle-class neighborhood? We just wanted to have normal problems like everyone else, and these problems were definitely not normal. Here it was the middle of the night and we were worried about creatures standing in a forest. I told Dean I wished we had never heard that howl, and he agreed. After a few more hours of talking, and checking the house repeatedly I was exhausted and emotionally drained. I guess I could have watched them again to see what they were doing, but I was too afraid because they were watching our house. I sat on the couch and closed my eyes for only a second and quickly fell asleep.

When morning arrived, I opened my eyes to find Dean sitting at the desk. He had stayed up all night to guard the house and watch me sleep. Things looked brighter in the morning. I felt a sense of great relief we had made it through the night with no incidents. Our darkest hour had passed and we were still OK. Maybe the large ones were here to stop the smaller ones from harming us, who knows? Still it was a tense situation and I told Dean no more placing bait or cameras in the forest. He agreed and said we would talk to Mr. Hill about it.

Soon the phone rang. It was Mr. Hill, and he would be arriving at any moment. If the camera was still there, we would see the Bigfoots on it. He also placed a recording device in the forest, and hopefully, it had worked and he had recorded them.

When Mr. Hill arrived, he went into the forest and came out with the camera. I met him on our porch and on the way into our house I asked him about the bait, and he said something had definitely gotten some of it. I also asked whether he saw any footprints as he walked into the forest. He had—some fresh prints near the entrance. When I asked how many, he didn't answer because I don't think he heard me. He was busy focusing on the camera. I didn't care because we were about to see up close pictures of the Bigfoots.

He sat down and began to look at the pictures.

"One raccoon, two raccoons, three raccoons, and then a cat with pictures of the forest with no animals in between," he recounted. "That's strange. I will have to go home and look at them on a larger screen because the camera should not have taken a picture of just the forest. Something has to activate the motion sensor."

He explained to us that when the camera sensed motion, it took a picture and then automatically took a second one. He was perplexed by all of the consecutive pictures of the forest showing nothing in it. I too was perplexed by the lack of findings.

"Are you sure you pointed the camera toward the entrance to the forest?" I asked.

"Oh, no," he said. "I placed it down the path at the fork on the trail, pointing at the fork."

I was shocked to find out that the camera was not pointed at the forest entrance. For sure the four large Bigfoots would have been on the camera since they were standing right there. I questioned him about why he didn't set the gaming camera to point on the path toward the entrance since that's where I had seen them repeatedly.

"Well," he replied, "I thought the flash might bother the cars as they drove by, and since the camera is motion activated, it would have also taken pictures of them."

My heart sank as I looked at the pictures of the fork because I knew that was not where they would be found, although he was right about the camera shooting pictures of cars as they drove by. Still I was extremely disappointed at not having a photo of the Bigfoots, but I thought maybe at least the sounds of them were recorded. Mr. Hill had to go, as he was investigating another case and said it was an emergency; the Bigfoots were threating a family by throwing large rocks at them. Dean and I just looked at each other and thought about, what that family must be going through, we certainly could sympathize. We figured we could talk to him later about what happened last night. I asked him to call after he examined the pictures and listened to the audio recording.

As we waited to here from Mr. Hill over the next few days, the Bigfoots returned, and I watched them again. Two were very active, jumping around a tree to the left of the forest entrance across from the streetlight. It looked like they were testing their strength by going up and down the tree trunk; they would take turns lifting and climbing on each other to reach a high branch. Once one was hanging from the branch, the other would hang from him and try to pull him down. The one hanging would purposely use only one arm. They had long arms, barrel bodies, and stubby-looking legs. Due to their behavior and size I assumed they were young ones.

There were also others in the forest, up the trees and along the path. I kept trying to get a better look at their faces because the thinner ones, average man size or smaller, appeared a little different from the larger ones. Also, some appeared to have pointy ears on the tops of their heads. It could just have been the way their hair was standing up on top of their heads that looked like ears, but I didn't think so. To me the images were confusing, and I was still trying to figure them out.

On November 29, I heard a knock at the front door. Surprisingly, it was Mr. Hill. I greeted him at the door and asked whether he had news regarding the audio recording and the pictures. He said he didn't but that he had other news for us and placed a printed report in my hand. At first I thought it was a sighting report from one of our neighbors, but instead it was an online report detailing the beginning of our investigation posted on a website for everyone to read.

"I'm sorry," he said, "but I can no longer officially continue the investigation since it has been posted online."

I was shocked and replied, "Who could have done this?"

"Read the posting and I will call you later," he said.

I quickly read the posting, and, to my dismay, Jack had written it. He had gone online to report about the Bigfoots across the street. He wrote about our discovering them and Mr. Hill's investigation. The report was only a few pages, but it detailed some of the evidence collected and even included a map illustrating the forest. Although our address was not listed and the streets were blurred out, I guess because of the map someone could research and find the location. His last posting was of the night Mr. Hill sat in the forest. It turned out his writing was very popular, and we had no idea he was doing it. Of course, we found all this out after having a conversation with him. His intent was not to compromise the investigation or do Mr. Hill's job; he just wanted to let people know about the Bigfoots. I guess his generation puts everything online. We immediately asked Jack to take down the posting, and he said he would try.

The next day I called Mr. Hill to apologize for what Jack had done. Mr. Hill explained why the posting was not a good idea.

"People could find the location, and pranksters could tamper with the evidence. But," he continued, "Jack did a good job of reporting, and I was impressed by his writing; maybe he should continue. Either way, I'm going to have to close my official investigation because of the online report."

It all made little sense to me, and I struggled to understand after few more minutes of talking he finally said, "The Bigfoots are there, and they aren't going anywhere and even though I can't officially continue to investigate, if you need me, I'm only a phone call away. Also, I have notified the local police department of their presence, just in case something happens or they see something in the forest. They need to know what they're dealing with. There's really nothing more I can do."

We certainly appreciated all that he had done, but I had thought he would do something to get rid of them. I wasn't really concerned about any report, official or otherwise; I was concerned about the Bigfoots.

"What are we going to do?" I asked him "I don't want to live with Bigfoots across the street from our house. What can we do to make them leave?"

"There's nothing you can do," he replied. "It's a male Bigfoot's territory and has been so for years; they're not going to leave."

I thought, "You've got to be kidding!" Honestly, I believed he could make them go away. Once we determined how many there were and what kind, I assumed he would know what to do about them. I couldn't believe what I was hearing: there was nothing we could do? After hanging up the phone, I had a deep feeling of despair and loneliness.

Now that I was completely disillusioned and frustrated, my emotions began to run wild, and the whole investigation started to seem pointless. Evidently, our fate was sealed from the very beginning, and we would no longer be able to live in peace. I didn't even know how to ignore them. Now that I knew they were there and had seen them, how was I ever going to sleep at night? It all seemed unfair. These Bigfoots were hiding in our forest, and we couldn't get rid of them, and yet it seemed like the whole world was searching for them. How ironic was that? I wanted to scream.

10

Adam's Mistake

Recent photo of view from master bedroom window

On November 30 at 8:35 p.m., the Bigfoots were out again and making a lot of noise, including tossing leaves and snapping branches. I really didn't want to watch them since it only caused more grief. We could do nothing about them, and I was only torturing myself by continuing to monitor the forest. I thought about turning off the volume and trying to ignore them—maybe that's what I should have done. But after I listened to them for a long time, curiosity got the best of me, and I could no longer concentrate on anything else. Their being so announcing was not normal; they were usually much quieter, and I wondered what they were doing. So, despite reservations, I drudgingly headed upstairs to see what was happening.

Dean was watching television in the family room, and all our sons were home for the night. I informed Dean about the Bigfoots being outside. I reflected back on how we used to spend our evenings together relaxing, making dinner, or sitting down to watch our favorite television shows. Boy, how our nights had changed! Adam met me in the hallway as I reached the top of the stairs. He wanted to talk about his girlfriend. I told him OK, but that there was a lot of noise outside and I needed to see what was happening. He decided to go with me and talk while I scoped through the window. After talking for a while, he asked me whether I saw anything.

"Yes," I answered. "I can see at least three Bigfoots in the forest and maybe one more standing in the shadows along the path to the left of the entrance behind a bush. I think he is probably the lookout for the others. I can see slight movement along the path in the bush every now and then. One I can clearly see is sitting down and leaning against a tree, next to some brush, to the right of the entrance path. He is on the edge of the forest doing something with his hands; it looks like he is playing with the freshly mulched grass on the easement. Your father mulched the easement yesterday. He is flicking the grass clippings into a pile using his fingertips of both hands at the same time, as a pastime, I assume, before falling sleep. Now I know how they form piles of leaves and grass clipping without leaving any marks on the ground.

"There's also at least two more lying in the forest next to him to the right," I continued. "They are lying along the forest bottom, maybe leaning their heads against the trees further in the forest. I can't really tell where one begins and the other ends or how many there are, so there could be more. They remind me of a pride of lions lounging after a hunt."

Adam asked to see them. I agreed and handed him the scope, as I reemphasized to him to move the curtains slightly. I again tried to give him directions of where to look in the forest. He struggled with my directions, and I struggled with his lack of patience. After a few minutes of searching, Adam couldn't find them, so I asked him to give back the scope so I could check to see whether they were still there. I looked again, and they were still there.

Perplexed as to why he couldn't spot them, I asked him what he was looking for. I thought he expected to see the creatures standing out in the open, flaying their arms and growling like on a television show. Of course, that not what you saw; if you didn't know what to look for, they were hard to spot, and you were lucky if you saw them moving outside the brush. Usually, they were hiding, and it was difficult to find them.

After lecturing Adam on how to spot Bigfoots in the forest, I noticed he wasn't really paying attention; he was busy texting his girlfriend on his cell phone. He started to leave the room when I noticed our car had a lot of light reflecting on the windshield. It looked like the dome light was on and maybe the door was ajar. I mentioned it to Adam, and said something about Dean checking the car later.

Unfortunately, that's not what Adam heard, so he decided to go outside and check the car. On this particular night, the car happened to be parked behind Adam's truck in the driveway. That put the car directly across from the forest entrance and less than thirty feet away from the Bigfoots.

I first noticed the front yard motion sensor lights went bright as I saw Adam emerging from underneath the roof of the front porch. Within seconds, he was standing alone at the edge of the street next to the car. Adam is a big guy who stood nearly six feet tall, so it took him only a few steps. I couldn't believe he had gone out the front door so quietly; I didn't even hear the door open or close, and I was standing directly above it on the second floor.

I began to panic, knowing that he was in danger of startling the Bigfoots. Dean and I had discussed the need to make lots of noise when going outside at night, so as not to do this. I guess we forgot to tell Adam. I thought, "Adam, just check the car and get back in the house." As I quickly looked through the night vision scope and scanned the forest, but it was too late. The Bigfoots were startled and immediately started to move. Yelling for Dean wasn't an option because he was on the other side of the house and wouldn't have heard me. I considered grabbing a gun, but it probably would have put Adam in more danger. All I could do was watch as the horrifying events unfolded.

Adam bent down to look in the car and then stood up, turned and faced the forest entrance, and took one step toward the street. He looked frozen, standing between the car and the mailbox and staring straight into the forest path. I immediately focused on the path and saw two large, round eyes peering at Adam. It was the lookout Bigfoot standing on the left side of the entrance. I could tell by the way he glared at Adam that he was not afraid of him. He didn't move or even try to hide. He just stood there staring at him. Adam didn't move, either; he stood there facing the creature. I couldn't believe what was happening, and I wanted Adam to run, but he never did. I felt completely helpless but thought somehow my watching him meant he wasn't alone.

Adam, without taking his eyes off the Bigfoot standing on the path slowly began to raise his right arm and pointed toward the right of the entrance. I quickly focused to the right and saw one of them rise out of the thicket and form a terrifying shape. It rose to all fours in a threating position with huge shoulders and a slopped back. His eyes reflected as he too glared at Adam. He emerged for only a few seconds and never stood upright, and then he slid smoothly back into the thicket and disappeared. By this time, the one along the path had also faded into the darkness. I didn't have enough time to focus on the others lying on the ground, but they too were gone. It was all over, and Adam was still in one piece.

Adam slowly came back into the house while still keeping an eye on the forest. My heart was racing as I quickly ran downstairs to meet him at the front door. He was a quite shaken and had a weird look on his face; it was expressionless, and his big brown eyes were wide open. He just stood there, unable to speak as he gathered his thoughts. I asked whether he was OK, and told him I had seen the whole event. He walked into the office and sat on the couch, still processing what happened. I ran to get Dean so Adam could tell us both what he had experienced.

His frightening story was as follows: "When I went outside to look in the car, I heard something moving behind me, in the bushes on the path, so I looked into the forest. I saw two eyes looking back at me, and I thought to myself, 'Oh, God, let that be a reflection from the leaves.' It just stared directly at me, and I could see him standing in the dark, and then he slowly walked away. I could hear his footsteps as he walked through the forest, stepping on the leaves."

Taking many factors into consideration, he began to estimate the size of the Bigfoot, such as his size and the elevation of the driveway compared to the forest floor and the height of the eyes. He said he had to have been at least eight feet tall.

"Why didn't you run back into the house?" I asked.

"It was like looking eye to eye with a wild animal," he said, "and I knew not to turn my back on him. That's why I stood there staring at him until he walked away. Really, there was nothing I could do; if he wanted to hurt me, he could have easily taken me out, but I thought not without a struggle."

"Why did you point?" I asked.

He quickly answered, "I pointed to the right because I heard a lot of noise—leaves moving and more walking sounds. I knew you were watching, so I wanted to let you know they were moving. I was too focused on the one staring at me."

"That's why I wanted your dad to check the car later and not you!" I said. "Your dad always opens the garage door and makes lots of noise, not to mention he's armed." I shook my head and continued, "You're lucky you didn't look to the right, because there was another one that rose out of the thicket, on all fours. He would have scared you beyond belief because he was a lot closer to you. He scared the heck out of me, and I was in the house."

He was quite affected by this experience, to have looked eye to eye with the beast and having heard the footsteps up close. After processing what happened, he was also somewhat jazzed by the experience. We talked about it for a while, and then he left to go tell Jack and William his hair-raising story while Dean and I stayed in the office and continued to talk about the evening's events. I was an emotional mess from all the excitement and just wanted the night to end. Watching Adam so close to several Bigfoots was more than I could handle, and we were very fortunate that he was not harmed. Adam was OK, and the Bigfoots were gone—or so we thought.

Unfortunately for us, the night was far from over, because while Dean and I were still talking in the office, Jack after hearing Adam's story wanted to calm the Bigfoots, by feeding them.

Adam in the meantime, was upstairs in our bedroom looking for them with the night vision scope.

Dean and I were completely stunned by the sound of the front door as it opened and closed. We both looked at the monitor and saw Jack running into the forest. He had grabbed a piece of leftover steak and hamburger patty with a napkin to feed the Bigfoots. I was extremely upset and yelled for Dean to catch him, but by the time Dean made it to the street, Jack was already returning from the forest. When they returned, I had a discussion with Jack about what he had done. Needless to say, it was a loud conversation, and I was not happy. He listened for a while and then left the room. Dean followed him to continue a much calmer conversation.

Meanwhile, Adam having watched Jack run into the forest to place the food, decided to focus on it. A few minutes later, the phone rang; I answered it, and to my surprise it was Adam calling from his cell phone upstairs.

"I saw the Bigfoot retrieving the food," he said. "his giant arm came out from the side of the path behind the bushes. It reached out very slowly, three times, until nothing was left. It was amazing to see his long arm and fingers. His reach was at least four to five feet."

"Great," I replied and hung up the phone. I was too upset with Jack for messing with the Bigfoots and really didn't want to hear any more about them.

Adam, still hyped from his sightings, came into the office and said, "I now understand how to use the scope to spot them. When you tell us to look at a certain spot, we need to stay focused on it for a long time to catch them. I was getting bored with watching the food and wanted to move the scope around, but something told me to stay focused on the food. I did, and eventually I saw his long, hairy arm and hand."

I know he was just trying to make me feel better because he had finally learned how to use the night vision scope, but it didn't work. I was so upset, and angry that I couldn't even speak. He sat with me for a few seconds and when I didn't respond, he left to go tell everyone else again what he had seen.

I just wanted this night to end. I had aged enough for one day. I decided to sit and watch television to clear my head and try to relax. I watched for many hours and then realized it was 3:15 a.m. everyone but Jack was asleep in the house; he was watching television with me and had just gone upstairs. Tired of watching television yet still unable to sleep, I decided to go back into the office to listen to some recordings. The sun would be coming up soon and it seemed like all the night's activities were finally over— or so I thought.

Weary from all that had happened, I abruptly walked back into the office and sat at the desk. I wasn't really paying attention to anything in particular when suddenly I smelled the most putrid odor. It was coming from somewhere near the window behind me. Immediately, I was wide awake and realized my mistake. Frightened, I couldn't get out of the chair fast enough and ran from the office. Fortunately, I ran into Jack in the kitchen; he had come back downstairs to get a snack. I quickly told him what happened and asked whether he could check it out. He went to the office and checked the monitors before turning on the additional front porch lighting and looking out the window. Terrified, I stood back in the hallway and watched.

"It's OK, Mom," he said, "I don't see anything."

Again, Jack has anosmia, so it was pointless to ask him about the stench. I slowly returned to the office, and the smell was gone. But I should have checked the monitor and the motion sensor lights around the front of the house before sitting at the desk. I also realized that having my back to the window was not a good idea, so Jack and I moved the desk and rearranged the office. The rest of the night, I watched the clock and waited for daylight. Thank goodness morning came quickly and the night was finally over.

A few days later, I listened to the audio recording from that night and I heard something terrifying. A Bigfoot was close to the front porch microphone at 3:11 a.m. It was growling and then swinging at something and seemed angry (Growl with Swishing).

I quickly realized that despite Mr. Hill closing his investigation, we still needed to protect our home by keeping an eye on the creatures. Now, due to the investigation, us chasing them through the forest, and Adam's sighting, they knew we were aware of them.

11

Disturbing Images

Bigfoot by fence, zoomed and contrasted.

As the sun rose, Dean was up early and decided to take me to breakfast. While driving home, I found myself looking out the car window and observing the forest along the side of the road. Here the forest was everywhere. I began to look for the signs of a Bigfoot presence: broken or peeled trees; bowed limbs with vines weaved through them to catch leaves and nettles as they fell, creating artificial camouflage for the Bigfoots to hide behind; mounds on the ground; or piles of leaves and branches. I knew what to look for, but I didn't know whether these indicators held true to all forests.

I told Dean as we drove by a neighborhood, "Look at all the bent trees—something very strong did that. That neighborhood probably has Bigfoots visiting their forest and they don't know it. Those families are living their lives, possibly being watched by the beast. He is watching their every move, eating out of their trash cans, sleeping in their sheds, and maybe eating their little pets. I know we see a lot of missing pet signs in our neighborhood; maybe they do too."

The drive should have been relaxing, but instead I had Bigfoots on my mind. I watched people in the cars as we drove by them. I thought about how too their lives would change, watching creatures day and night in a forest, seeing what was not meant to be across the street from their houses. Would they be able to forget about it and function, pretend that it wasn't happening? It's one thing to tell someone we had Bigfoots across the street from our house and another to watch them. Any person would question his or her sanity. I grew weary of watching these creatures in the forest among other things. It all just made no sense.

Shortly after arriving home, I noticed movement again in the forest by Steve and Becky's house. I had been observing the forest and constantly looking for the daytime Bigfoot and kept seeing strange images of creatures similar in color to him. However, the images were confusing, and at this point I didn't know what to think of them. Some creatures I saw were small and scary looking, and their hands seemed to have claws. I was taking lots of pictures, so I hoped to have captured something;

however, the camera was not for distant or moving objects, so it was very frustrating. Every time I tried to zoom in on them, the pictures pixelated and lost focus. After watching all the strange activity occurring in the forest I couldn't help but wonder has it always been this way? Had they been there for years during the day as well as at night?

Later that evening, at 9:49 p.m., they arrived again, and I reluctantly watched them. Strangely, only two were on the forest path: one on the right of the path and the other on the left. The branches were moving a lot, and I could hardly see them, making out only their arms as they moved the trees. Because of all the movement, I got the feeling that something was happening farther down the path along the sides of it.

I kept focusing down the path to see what was happening, when all of a sudden two kittens came into view. I didn't know to whom they belonged or where they came from; they just appeared in the night vision scope. They were approaching the forest entrance where the two Bigfoots were along the path. I panicked and thought, "Watch out, little kittens! They're right there!" but they scampered into the forest, past the Bigfoots, and became absorbed by darkness. I was horrified and worried about the kittens, but there was nothing I could do. I thought, "Just great, another disturbing image to live with." I had seen other disturbing things that I didn't want to write about.

Later that evening I went to watch the creatures again and look for the kittens. Instead, outside of the forest to the left of the entrance, I saw a whole Bigfoot squatting down on the easement in front of the thicket with his long arms in front of him, touching the ground. Seeing him completely out in the open was very surprising. He was looking around and eating something, bending his arm inward and raising his hands to his mouth. I watched as he kept moving his head back and forth, observing his surroundings. With broad shoulders, thick-looking arms, and a slender body, he was much smaller than the other Bigfoots I had seen; maybe he was a young one. His jaw was protruding, and I saw what looked like ears on the top of his head? I watched him for quite a while. Behind him, just inside the thicket, others were hiding and scratching a tree. I could see their movement, but I tried to stay focused on the one in the open. I kept waiting for a car to drive by to see whether he would go back into the forest, but no luck. He just stayed there.

Eventually, I became tired of watching. The scope got heavy after a few minutes, and my eyes became strained. Also for some reason, I become physically ill when observing them. This happened a lot when I watched them, so I could watch only a few minutes at a time. My stomach always hurt and my body felt strained. It was very painful, and even though I was getting used to watching them, it didn't get any easier.

12

Dark Camera

View from the office window

On December 3, we purchased an outdoor night vision camera. With this camera placed outside, we would be able to watch the Bigfoots on a television screen in the office. No longer would I suffer watching them alone, going up and down the stairs all night in the dark in fear of being seen. We would now be able to track their whereabouts from the moment they arrived without causing a lot of stress. The camera was supposed to have a sixty-foot range at night. In order to conceal the camera and get it as close to the street as possible without looking out of place, we decided to hide it in the front yard Christmas decorations. Our decorations consisted of a large wooden sleigh with five reindeer and several candy canes, along with other yard ornaments.

We attached the camera to one of the wooden candy canes and strung Christmas lights around it to conceal the red glowing lights surrounding the camera lens. These glowing lights produced the infrared (IR) light radiating from the camera that allowed it to view at night. The IR light was invisible to humans, but some animals could see it. The wooden candy cane was approximately fifteen feet from the street in the center of our front yard. The street was twenty-five feet wide, and the easement was ten feet. So with the sixty-foot range, we would easily see the part of the forest where the Bigfoots usually hide. We focused the camera directly on the forest path. It had a wide lens and could view at least thirty feet of the forest front. We linked the camera to a television screen with a VHS recorder, in hopes of capturing them on tape. It took us all afternoon to setting up the camera because we also had to decorate the front yard for Christmas; we finished at dusk.

We were curious to see the images produced by the camera. Immediately, we had some type of condensation bubble forming on the camera, causing it to white out part of the lens. Dean went outside to wipe it with a rag, and this worked for a while, but then it returned. We thought it was from the humidity. Despite this problem, we could see the forest, but when the camera changed from day to night, the forest also changed.

The bushes and trees appeared thicker, and the forest was full of strange, dark images with ghastly shapes. Since the camera viewed in shades of black and white at night, we suspected that the shadows and the trees were layering to form these images. The withering tree branches looked like arms attached to strange bodies. We saw large, dark silhouettes of things between the trees with reflecting eyes—some of them could have been Bigfoots. Who really knew for sure? When the wind blew, everything moved, including the images with the reflecting eyes.

Some of frightening images were of ghostly things such as faces peeking from the bushes or bodies with no heads. We were not looking for ghosts, but seeing these things scared me. Ghost hunters would have gone nuts over here—it was a complete freak show.

I asked Dean jokingly, "Whose idea was this?"

As we watched the camera, things continued to appear and disappear. Many sets of eyes were peeking high and low. Some of the images didn't move and it was like watching a still photo of something creepy. Even more disturbing, some did move.

What the hell was wrong with this camera? Why was it picking up so many ghoulish images? I had seen some strange ghostly things in the forest but not this many. It seemed like every creepy thing in the forest appeared that night to see the Christmas decorations. We couldn't tell what was real. After watching a while, Dean gave up trying to decipher the images, so he left the room. I watched in horror for a few hours while trying to make sense of what I was seeing. The light was bouncing everywhere, and it created a lot of static that distorted the images even more. It seemed the only way to confirm these images were real was to use the night vision scope. Disappointed, I headed upstairs to scope the forest again, questioning why people bought those cameras.

After placing the scope to my eye, I slowly began to pull back the curtain when suddenly a bright flash of light reflecting through the scope nearly blinded me. It was like being hit with a flash camera. I lowered the scope and blinked several times, attempting to regain my vision. I thought, "What the heck just happened?" So I pulled back the curtain and looked out the window.

The front yard spotlights around the Christmas sleigh were pointed toward the house, producing a blinding glare on the window. We were so concerned about hiding the camera we didn't realize how many lights were in the front yard. I couldn't see anything across the street. We had no way to confirm whether the large images appearing on the fixed night vision camera were indeed Bigfoots. What a huge oversight. After calming down, I headed back downstairs to the office, disappointed in how the evening was developing. The night vision camera produced a cluster of creatures. It was ridiculous to think all these strange things were actually there. I was completely inexperienced at identifying things in the forest at night using that camera.

I knew some of the images had to have been Bigfoots because we recorded another childlike voice, and this time it said, "Mommy and mother," along with something else we couldn't make out (Mimic #3).

Not wanting to move the camera I watched it a few more days, but still the images weren't becoming any clearer. At night, the images of the forest continued to be frightening, full of ghostly things with reflecting eyes. Even during the day, the camera had poor resolution and couldn't project exactly what the forest looked like. I also reviewed the VHS tapes, and they were full of static and blurred images. Having the camera pointed directly at the forest seemed to be a mistake.

13

Our Neighbor's Window

View of our neighbor's window from William's office

After a week of watching the camera and seeing the most horrific things, we decided to move it away from the street. I didn't want the camera pointed directly at the forest anymore. We placed it in a planter box up against our fence in the front of our house. This helped to make the camera's bright light less conspicuous at night. We could now turn off the Christmas lights at 10:00 p.m. so I could use the night vision scope later if needed. We repositioned the camera to view across our front lawn, down the street to the left of our house, and along the forest front. We figured by turning the camera that way we would have an unobstructed view if any Bigfoots crossed the street or approached the house at night.

On the afternoon, of December 8, the neighborhood children were noisily playing ball in the street one house away from Steve and Becky's home. I could see them on the stationary night vision camera as I worked in the office. I wasn't really paying attention to the camera screen since I figured with all the noise the Bigfoots would naturally stay hidden. When I couldn't hear the children anymore, I glanced up at the camera and noticed dark images forming in the forest next to Steve and Becky's house.

The images moved slightly and looked suspicious because they were piling along the edge of the forest near the street. Soon it was dark, and more images began to appear, and then the creepy ones showed up. Immediately, I thought the camera was again creating these images, caused by the trees overlapping and the leaves reflecting in the streetlight. Disappointed, I quickly dismissed them.

As the night continued, I watched the images with little interest until I noticed that the window light on the side of Steve and Becky's house was changing. The window was a standard four-by-four square facing the forest, but you could also see it from the street. They had a six-foot wooden fence around that side of the house that ended at the forest edge. I could clearly see the shape of the window from a distance because it was emitting light.

I watched as parts of the window would slowly disappear and then reappear again. It looked as if shadowy figures were blocking the light and moving back and forth. After watching this happen for more than an hour, I determined the trees simply blowing in the wind could not have caused this unusual activity; something solid had to be blocking the light. Shockingly, these were real images I was viewing through the night vision camera.

In order to investigate what was happening, I grabbed the night vision scope and went upstairs to William's office. It sat on the second floor on the side of our garage. From his office window, I could view the neighborhood to the left of our house, which included the street and Steve and Becky's home. When I first looked out our window into our neighbors' yard, I could see the moving shadows because of the streetlight and our garage lights. They appeared as dark outlines of hairy creatures shaped like Bigfoots. Some were in their yard and at the forest edge. The ones in their yard were gathering outside their window and trying to look into their children's playroom. I knew that window was to their children's playroom because a few years ago Steve and Becky added on to their home and I was invited to see the finished construction.

After watching them using just my eyes, I tried to use the night vision scope to see detail. However, seeing any details of the dark images was not possible. I wasn't able to use the night vision scope because of all the light. I ended up watching them for quite a while until my eyes gave out trying to verify what I was seeing. It was all so strange because it also looked like there were smaller ones on their roof. It was all unbelievably disturbing, and I didn't know what to do.

I went back downstairs and sat quietly in the office while still watching their window on the night vision camera as the light kept changing. This was a shocking development. How do you tell someone, that you suspected there were Bigfoots in their yard at night, peeking through their window and climbing on their roof?

Especially when they don't know anything about them, Steve and Becky seemed to be a happy young couple, with two active seven-year-old twins. It would certainly change their lives forever—and not for the better. I, for one, knew this firsthand. I was afraid to let our dogs out at night; I couldn't imagine raising two young children next to this forest.

Would they even believe me? I guess I could show them the evidence along with the recording of their window light vanishing at night, but could they handle it? I could barely handle it, and it was not my house. As long as they were happy, did they really have to know everything? We lived here seven years without knowing and I was happier. Now I stayed up at night and my life was in turmoil as a result of constantly tracking the Bigfoots. I quickly learned that once you knew of them, there was no turning back, and it affected everything around you. This news could destroy their happy family so I had to contemplate what to do.

14

Mysterious Red Eyes

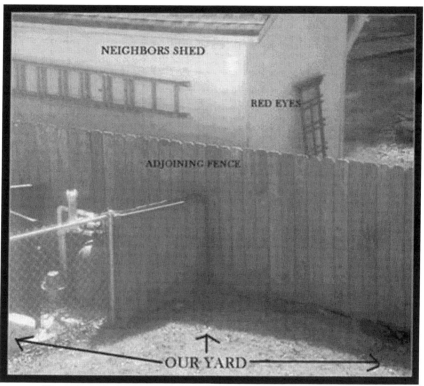

Daytime window view of shed and adjoining fence

We recorded another childlike voice calling out in the night as it wandered through the neighborhood. It said "Mommy" several times at 11:37 p.m. (Mimic #4). I kept wondering about this childlike voice and why it kept calling for its mommy. Then it dawned on me, most people would think it was a helpless child, lost and confused. I remembered watching old horror movies, where something calls out using an innocent voice, when they go outside to see what it is they meet their demise. Was this creature trying to bait me?

After watching our neighbors' window for a few nights and not seeing the Bigfoots across from our house, we relocated the night vision camera to get a closer look at the forest next to Steve and Becky's house. That side of the forest had fewer trees and lower bushes behind a shallow thicket. Dean moved the camera first thing in the morning to the far side of our garage and pointed it directly at the forest. Within hours of placing the camera, in broad daylight, the dark images began to appear.

Fortunately, it was daytime, so I grabbed the handheld camera and headed for the family room window that sat directly across from that side of the forest. The forest appeared odd, as if the patterns on the bushes were out of place and the colors didn't match. I got the impression that something was camouflaged hiding in the bushes. I could see glimpses of the creatures I called the daytime Bigfoots. I got the feeling they were bad news, aggressive and dangerous.

I kept seeing images of a beastly face. Something was definitely not right about them and it was concerning me. Their behavior was very strange; I found it hard to imagine that Mr. Hill would want to sit in a forest at night waiting to meet them. They didn't seem at all friendly. After watching them for a while, I began to take pictures, but they noticed me and disappeared into the forest. This seemed to happen a lot when I tried to take pictures of them. Sometimes when I saw them, I got so frustrated with the camera that I wanted to run outside to get a picture. I think I did once or twice however; something told it was a mistake, based on the images I was seeing. It was best to be cautious and stay away from the forest when they were there.

Later that evening, more unexplained things began to show up on the night vision camera. Pointing the camera at the forest just seemed pointless since I always saw hideous things with eyes moving around. I quickly became bored with it and didn't like watching the images. That night as I sat in the office, I wondered, "If the Bigfoots are in one neighbor's yard, climbing on their roof and looking through their window, how many others are they invading at night?" I already suspected they were getting close to our house due to the audio recordings, but what about our backyard and our adjoining neighbors houses.

I decided to investigate by looking out the windows at the back of our house from the second floor. From this elevation, I could easily see the neighborhood behind us and the houses of our neighbors who share our fence. We had porch lights all around the back of our house and on the sides, so it was easy to see our yard, and it appeared normal. Yet when I viewed the back fence line of our next-door neighbors' yard, I saw a suspicious silhouette of a Bigfoot towering over their back fence next to a tree. Due to its lack of movement and distance, I had no way to confirm it. However, in the morning, I could see nothing there that would have formed that image, and I never saw it again.

Over the next few days, I continued observing the neighborhood and the yards behind our house. One night, my eye caught something moving directly behind us in in our neighbors' backyard. It passed by in a flash, and I thought, "What the heck was that?"

I saw red eyes moving through the darkness. At first I thought it was a raccoon or possum running across the top of our adjoining six-foot wooden fence. But there were other flashes of red eye shine occurring sporadically throughout their backyard and beyond the fence. There was enough light from our porch and theirs that I could see the eye flashes but couldn't make out the shadowy figures creating them.

In the distance, something large was standing just within the shadows of our neighbors' emitting porch light, toward the right side of their elevated porch below their French-door windows that were not covered. All the light made it impossible to use the night vision scope. However, I was able to use the binoculars to see the eyes closest to our fence by our neighbors' shed. Their shed sat directly along the fence to the left of our house. A pair of red eyes reflected from the shadow of it two feet above the fence, looking at back of our house. I could see the flashes of one eye and then the other.

"What the heck are you?" I thought, "And why are your eyes reflecting red?" It was chilling to watch them, and no matter how hard I tried, I couldn't positively identify the creatures.

I also noticed movement in the neighbors' corner tree it sat next to the fence on the right. The tree appeared unusually thick—like a dark mass with no light shining through it, not even the moonlight. However, there were flickers of light in it, that at the time, I discounted as leaf shine because I was busy watching the red eye flashes below it.

It was 2:30 in the morning, and I noticed Adam's room light was still on. I quietly knocked on his door and asked whether he wanted to see something strange. He said he would but to give him a minute. He stopped his game on the computer and met me in the hallway. I quickly explained to him what was happening as we both enter the dark, spare bedroom and I handed him the binoculars. As he looked out the bedroom window, he said he could see the red eyes reflecting and moving through the yard and agreed they were strange looking. I asked whether he could make out the creatures. He watched for a few more minutes through different sides of the window in hopes of getting a better look.

"No, I can't see what they look like," he finally replied. "Do you want me to go outside and shoot them with a flashlight?"

I whispered, "No! You can't go shooting a flashlight in the neighbor's yard at 2:30 in the morning! Besides, we don't know what they are? They could be Bigfoots or something else, and they could get angry and come over that fence."

"Well, that's the only way you're going to know for sure," he said.

"I know," I said, "but I don't want you outside with them."

He went back to his room, but told me he would be up a few more hours if I needed him, disappointed that I didn't want him outside with a flashlight.

I didn't think our sons fully understood what I was going through and the amount of fear involved. After watching these Bigfoots for a while, to me they were terrifying and dangerous. Not to mention big and strong, basically a deadly combination of a prehistoric beast with intelligence. I only watched them because of my fear.

I suspected it was their red eyes I had seen, but I couldn't be sure, since I had never seen red eyes before. But what I did know for sure was shooting a flashlight at them and making threating gestures could be the end of us.

I watched a while longer until my eyes gave out and then I went to bed, not wanting to see anymore creepy things that night. Still wide awake, I laid there thinking about all the creepy things in the neighborhood that I saw at night because I was awake looking for them. Most people sleep unaware of what could be lurking in the darkness around their houses or peeking through their windows. I used to be one of them, and I think I was better off not knowing.

The next morning, I went out to investigate the backyard. I was shocked from the moment I saw the tree. It had five branches with ten leaves—literally a stick with a few leaves, not the thick tree I saw the night before. I should have seen ample moonlight through the limbs and all the way up the tree. I figured there had to be footprints around it and along the fence, especially near the shed. So I peeked through the wooden fence slats into our neighbors' yard.

To my surprise and dismay, all I saw was decorative rock along the fence line and encircling the tree. I climbed up on a box near the fence to look over hoping to find something. I noticed they had a lot of empty bird feeders in their yard, I counted seven. It made me wonder, do Bigfoots eat bird seed? With no footprints to be found, I had no evidence of the Bigfoots in their yard.

I went back into the house and thought about what to do next. Suddenly, I realized that I had finally found the perfect use for the night vision camera. It should be able to view our back fence without forming the creepy images. I could simply video above our fence at night and catch the Bigfoots standing next to it. Dean moved the camera and placed it on our side porch, angled to view our back fence and the corner tree. We were very careful not to video directly in our neighbors' backyard, even though I suspected the Bigfoots were there that night. We felt it would be improper to do so.

When the camera switched from day to night, I began to receive the ghostly images. Two of them had dark, cone-shaped heads with shoulders towering over the fence. It was the way they all of a sudden showed up and their lack of movement that made them suspicious, not likely to be real, solid images. However, the most frightening image was that of a white floating head above the fence with the most horrible expression. I thought one of our neighbors' yard decorations must have been reflecting in the camera—at least I hoped so.

The camera disappointed me again because it was producing freaky images so strange that we had to discount them. However, before we could adjust the camera or see what was causing the ghastly reflecting images, the screen went completely blank. "What the heck just happened?" I thought as I fiddled with the wires in the back of the television screen. When I couldn't get it to work again, I called for Dean to check the camera.

Dean went outside and quickly returned holding the camera with the cable line hanging from it and said, "I think Heidi bit the line in two. I guess she didn't like the camera, either."

I was disheartened that I could no longer capture the Bigfoots on video at night, but after seeing the frightening images again, I wasn't going to fix the camera anytime soon.

15

Untold Burden

Peeled tree

On December 14, we put everything on hold. William was graduating college on December 20, and my mother, aunt, and nephew were flying in early from California. They planned to be at the graduation and stay for a few days. I, of course, had been communicating with my mom and dad, telling them about the Bigfoots and what had been happening to us, but the rest of the family was unaware. All the plane tickets had been purchased prior to the discovery of the beasts. I didn't want to frighten them during their stay or distract from William's graduation, so we hid any signs of our monitoring of the creatures.

At first, it was difficult not staying up all night to listen for them and worrying about their lurking around the house. I informed our guests to close the windows at night and make sure the curtains were pulled tight. Thank goodness they didn't ask any questions. However, they probably noticed I looked tired and stressed. My mother was very helpful and supportive in keeping things normal since she knew why we were distracted.

I was so thankful for my parents, and although they were no longer together, I talked to both of them at least once a week. Discussing with them what we were going through comforted me because they lightened the mood by making me laugh. I always felt better after talking to both of them. I guess knowing I wasn't alone helped. They showed a true interest not only in what was happening to us but also in the Bigfoots. Through our experiences with the creatures, my father learned a lot about them and told me strange things that happened to him during his hunting days.

My father had hunted his whole life and spent a lot of time in the forest in several states where Bigfoots had been sighted. He told me a story that had forever bewildered him. He was hunting in Pagosa Springs, Colorado; he had hunted there every season for 10 years even though he lived in California. He and his friends would often go during the elk season in November. One day, he was all alone two miles deep into the forest and sitting along a ridge overlooking a canyon. Behind him, the mountain continued upward full of tall scrub oak and withering trees. He was hiding behind the tall scrub oak, sitting at the edge of the ridge, when all of a sudden he heard footsteps moving toward him from behind.

"It was very dry that year," he said, "and the leaves along the forest bottom made a loud crunching sound when you walked on them."

Assuming it was another hunter because the footsteps sounded like a person walking through the leaves, he stood up to announce his presence and greet the other hunter. However, when he looked over the tall scrub oak at the mountain behind him, he saw no one.

"Everything was still and quiet," he said.

So he dismissed the sounds and sat back down behind the tall scrub oak. He sat for only a few minutes when he heard the footsteps again but even louder, crushing through the leaves.

"It wasn't a bear," he stated, "because the sounds were of two feet walking, and I know what a bear sounds like."

He stood up again to see what hunter was making the noise, and scaring off the prey. Also he wanted the other hunter to know he was there because he didn't want to get shot by mistake.

"The moment I stood up, it went completely silent and I could see no one," he recounted. "Whatever it was, it was watching me because it stopped walking every time I stood up."

When it happened for the final time, he noticed dusk was upon him. He could see the bright orange sun setting over the mountain top. Perfect timing, he thought. He had already decided to get the hell out of there. Even though he had his rifle and wasn't overly afraid, he knew something was watching him, and he felt uneasy. On his way back to the campsite, he stood on top of the last ridge and looked down at the lights from all the campers. He had only the light of his flashlight to help guide him down the mountain to them. Looking behind him at the dark mountain range, he saw no other flashlight, so he knew that it was not a person stalking him.

"In all my years of hunting, I never once thought of a Bigfoot," he said. "It just never crossed my mind. But reflecting back, there were strange things that happened with no explanation."

After a few days of my family visiting, we were out shopping, eating, and relishing in the holiday season. Time seemed to fly by, and soon it was the day of William's graduation. He was the epitome of tall, dark, and handsome in his cap and gown. It was an overwhelming sight, a delightful time of joy and celebration. After the graduation, we celebrated at his favorite restaurant with family and friends. At dinner, I observed the people around us enjoying life as it should be—eating, smiling, and laughing.

I felt a deep sadness and really missed my life before the discovery of the Bigfoots. I felt like the whole world was rotating around me as I watched from a distance, shattered by the horrors I tracked at night. Our son's graduation should have been one of the highest points in my life, yet there I sat with the dark cloud on my shoulder, knowing that nightmares are real. I thought about Mr. Hill and others who pursued the unknown. What a burden they too must carry in knowing the truth. It was a much needed break and I thought maybe I should stop looking out the windows at night since it only caused me more grief.

On December 23, we returned from the airport after saying good-bye to my family. When we arrived home, the break was over—it was back to our bizarre reality. I decided to go through some of pictures we had taken. Although I had been viewing them periodically, I hadn't really zoomed in all of them yet. In addition, I also had more recordings to go through.

Soon the sounds of several tree limbs breaking echoed through the forest. I knew the Bigfoots were back across the street. The sounds were all there, and they seemed close because the motion sensor lights kept activating.

At 10:40 p.m., I noticed a large shadow near the front porch. Too scared to look out the window, I watched it for a while to see whether it moved. Dean was asleep, and I was alone in the office. After having watched many shadows at night, I really hated them because they too seemed strange, and they could come from anywhere and naturally move with the night. The shadow continued to look suspicious, moving only slightly. It was making me uncomfortable, so I had no choice but to look out the window. I thought about waking up Dean or one of our sons but I figured it was probably just a harmless shadow. When I finally got up the nerve, my heart was pounding. I had to take a moment to prepare myself and gather my thoughts of what to do if it was a Bigfoot. Do I run, grab the camera, or scream? Those were my choices. I also had the gun nearby just in case. I decided to grab the camera. I had been practicing how to use it at night to photograph through the front window. I prepared the camera by turning off the flash and then slowly pulled back the corner of the privacy shade. Holding back my fear, I peeked out the window and quickly looked at the shadow, knowing that whatever was out there probably had a clear view of me. I hoped it didn't want to be seen and would hide.

To my great relief, everything looked normal, and the shadow was nothing to worry about. It was being caused by the garage sensor light on the far corner of the house casting on the Christmas decorations. Still, something was activating that light, but I had no cameras on that side of the house. I sat back down at the desk and continued listening to the forest. I heard subtle sounds of something sneaking around outside: a snap, a click, and then tapping. Soon, the calm ended with a loud bang that sounded like someone hitting a metal shed. It was so loud that it woke up Dean and the dogs. I could hear them coming down the staircase quickly as they ran into the office to check on me. Dean asked whether I was OK, and the dogs were jumping around, anxiously wanting to go outside. It was late, so we decided to let them out after they calmed down, hoping this would prevent them from barking.

However, this was not what happened. Instead, we ended up recording the following event of a Bigfoot tormenting our dogs (Response). Dean and I were in the kitchen making a snack, so we did not hear the Bigfoot near the fence; we heard only the dogs barking. Only after listening to the recording did we hear the strange cries of the Bigfoot.

A lot was happening in the recording. Our dogs Foxy, Rocky, and Heidi were outside barking at the Bigfoot. Our dog Cockapoo was in the house next to the recording device. She heard what was happening outside and also barked and growled. The Bigfoot, I assume, was near the fence by the front door because it sounded close to the microphone. It cried out a weird, disturbing sound. The dogs began barking more aggressively, and the Bigfoot cried out again, using a one-syllable sound followed by a knock. The dogs moved away from the Bigfoot and went around the house to the back door. On the tape I could hear Heidi bark once in the distance followed by an unusual mock bark closer to the microphone, as if the Bigfoot was taunting the dogs.

Also in the recording were strange, haunting whispers in between the constant barking. The strange whispering voice said "Jenny" toward the beginning of the tape and then "Hide" (Response Jenny-Hide). We didn't know what to make of this voice, and we didn't know anyone named Jenny. It could have been a Bigfoot whispering or something else. Unfortunately for us, other things were lurking in the neighborhood, and I saw them too while tracking the Bigfoots at night.

16

Snow Blight

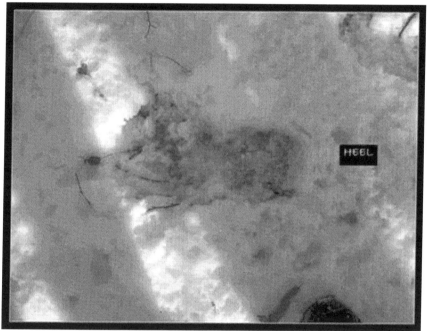

Bigfoot footprint in snow

Christmas Day 2012 was supposed to be a joyous occasion, but that year a snowstorm hit the state and knocked out power to more than half of the population. Our power was off for more than 24 hours. That night, as the snow fell, I could easily see the Bigfoots in the forest because the snow wasn't sticking to them. Some were standing under the trees while the smaller ones were sitting in them, causing the snow to fall off their limbs. It looked as if they were gathering near the edge of the forest, perhaps fascinated by the lack of lights in the neighborhood. I watched them as they moved freely through the forest, with their massive bodies darkening the pathways underneath the trees. As we sat with only the light from our lanterns and fireplace to keep us warm, I thought about our situation. Many people suffered through the challenges of having no power, but how many also had to worry about being surrounded by creatures that thrived in the night?

After a long and stressful night, the snow had finally stopped and the forest looked shattered. The weight of ice had caused the trees to collapse. That morning everything was covered in more than a foot of snow. By afternoon the sun was finally out and the snow was starting to melt. Soon thereafter we had our power restored. Having not seen any signs of the Bigfoots all morning, I was anxious to go into the forest and look for footprints before they melted. Dean and I threw on our coats and cautiously made our way toward the forest entrance. As we crossed the street, we noticed our neighbors and their children playing in the snow. They were making giant snowmen and throwing snowballs at each other in front of their houses.

When we finally made it to the forest entrance, what we saw was devastating. The broken and collapsed trees were everywhere; the entire path was buried. Large chucks of ice were melting from the tree tops and falling all around us, making it dangerous to walk under them. The frozen limbs were also cracking and falling.

We navigated around the fallen debris and immediately found the footprint of a Bigfoot. It looked fresh because not a lot of snow had fallen in it. We cautiously looked for more and attempted to follow them. Farther down the path, the tracks became harder to recognize. The snow was melting, and debris from the trees was obscuring the prints. We quickly realized that tracking was more difficult than we had imagined, because we had no clue which way the Bigfoot was traveling. By the time we reached what used to be the fork in the path, the snow was melted and patchy looking. To the left of the path, we could see no footprints traveling through that side of the forest. To the right it was blocked by broken and collapsed trees, we decided explore that route. I tied up my long hair and zipped up my coat as Dean pulled back the branches and held up the trees so I could crawl underneath them to the other side. There I saw more bent trees and broken branches covered in snow. I looked around but could not find more footprints. Ahead the forest looked destroyed, and the silence was creepy. Only the sound of the snow falling from the tree tops filled my ears.

I knew about the deep ditches on the sides of the path, because this section reminded me of a small bridge. Large drainage pipes ran underneath so the water runoff from the street could reach the creek. The edges of the path on both sides were hidden by fallen trees and bent branches topped with snow, so I went only a few feet because the ground seemed unstable. After snapping a few pictures, I had the strange feeling that something was watching me from underneath the collapsed branches covering the edge. Underneath, the color appeared abnormal. I walked closer and tried to get a better view, not realizing how close I was to the edge.

Suddenly, someone grabbed my shoulder and pulled me back. It was Dean; he had gotten past the debris and was standing behind me.

"What are you doing?" he asked in an alarming tone. "The edge is right there. Let's go back; it's too dangerous."

So we gave up exploring that side of the forest, but at least we had pictures of the Bigfoot footprints. When we got back to the house, I downloaded the photographs onto the computer and studied them right away. I could see two suspicious-looking dark images under the snow by the edge of the path. One was small and looked like an angry facial expression. The other looked like some type of expression with teeth. Both were disturbing to me. I showed the pictures to Jack but he said it could just be the debris forming these images, but I didn't think so.

As darkness fell on the second night, my fears came rushing back again as I wondered what the creatures were doing with no people or cars in sight. It was very cold and isolated due to the fallen snow. The night seemed very long, and I was up looking for them, but to my surprise, they didn't return.

After not having seen them for a few days I contacted Mr. Hill to check on him after the snow storm and tell him about the Bigfoot footprints in the snow. I figured he would be interested in them. He seemed happy to hear from us and said he would stop by and look at the photos.

Later that day he stopped by it was good to see him again and we had certainly missed his expert guidance. Updating him on all that had happened since the last time we had seen him would have taken hours, so instead we focused on the footprints. He studied the pictures and agreed that they were Bigfoot prints. I commented that I used the night vision scope and saw many of them on the first night of the snow but after that they were gone. I was hoping to get a lot more footprints when the snow stopped. However, I suspected it was too cold for their feet.

"No," he said, "it was not too cold for their feet. They know not to walk in the snow because they will leave footprints."

He said he should have been there right after the snow but he too had electrical problems. To investigate for himself, he went into the forest and returned later, telling us that he found Bigfoot tracks along the sides of the creek.

"They step in the water of the creek when the level is high," he explained. "When the water recedes, it uncovers their tracks."

He again attempted to follow the tracks, but the forest was nearly impossible to navigate due to all the storm damage. Before he left, I quickly mentioned to him our experiences involving the night vision camera and all the creepy images we had seen. I asked whether he had ever pointed a night vision camera into the forest. He said he knew what I was talking about; he too had seen some really strange things at night while using a night vision camera. I asked him how do you tell their Bigfoots, and he explained matter-of-factly that we should mark a couple of trees around seven feet high with two pieces of reflecting tape spaced about four inches apart; that way, anything that showed up with eyes at about the same height and width was determined to be a Bigfoot. I thanked him for the information but told him I would have to think about it, because I didn't want to see anymore ghostly images.

17

Disenchanted

Deer on easement at night

As the snow continued to melt, the forest was amazingly quiet. We heard no sound of anything moving through it. The storm debris was everywhere, making it impossible to see into the forest; even the entrance was buried under broken and collapsed trees.

We decided it was time to put away all the Christmas decorations. I told Dean that with the ornaments gone, we should have less shadows on the porch at night. It felt good to be outside without the feelings of being watched. I couldn't see that far into the forest, but what I did see appeared normal. There were no dark shadows or curious-looking images reflecting through it. I mentioned to Dean my concerns about the beasts returning.

"Well, maybe they won't return—at least not right away," He said. "I have been wondering why they were here. I think that maybe they were here due to the hunting season."

"I don't know much about the hunting season?" I said, "but something has changed, because the forest does seem vacant."

"Deer and other animals move into the housing areas during the season," he explained. "They know people can't shoot them near the houses. Maybe the creatures were following their food source. That's why they were in the neighborhood during this time of the year. It's quite possible they are not here year-round."

I certainly felt comforted by his words. I said, "Well, only time will tell whether your theory is correct and the creatures are indeed gone."

Without having to worry about the Bigfoots being here, I was able to focus on other things. Something was still bothering me about the daytime Bigfoots, and I needed to finish going through the pictures. They were frightening, dangerous, and aggressive, it seemed. I kept picturing the disturbing images of them, and they reminded me of something else. Not really knowing what the "type 2" Bigfoots should look like, I wondered whether these were the creatures Mr. Hill was referring to. He had never really told us much about them, so I decided to ask him and hopefully clear up some of my confusion. Since he was very helpful before and even stopped by, I was less apprehensive to ask him.

After reaching him by phone, I began to describe the daytime Bigfoots in detail, along with some of their behavior. He listened very carefully asked a few pointed questions. I answered them, and his voice changed to a tone of concern.

"I'm going to send you a link to a website," he said. "Watch the video then call me back and let me know whether this is what you are seeing."

After receiving his e-mail and visiting the site, I was shocked to find that what I had seen was a different type of creature. I couldn't believe what I was watching—they were describing the daytime Bigfoots. I quickly yelled for Dean to come into the office and also view the link. Most of what they described was what I had told Dean and my father about them.

Now horrified again, I told Dean, "You've got to be kidding me; the creature I saw during the day and sometimes at night, with pointed ears, is called a dog-man beast. What the hell is wrong with this forest, how many creepy things are in it?"

"You were right," Dean said. "They were something else."

I had begun to suspect that two separate species were in the forest because some of the nighttime ones were noticeably larger and had longer hair. I had hoped the others were adolescents and just hadn't yet developed into full-grown adults, but I was wrong. They were all terrifying to watch, and I did notice other differences between the two. Now it made sense! No, wonder why some had ears on the tops of their head.

After getting over the initial shock, I called Mr. Hill back to give him the bad news. I told him the creatures described were very similar to the daytime Bigfoots; however, the face was a little different. They did have snouts, but they were not as long as the drawings on the link. Other than that the description was correct. They were muscular and thin, less than six feet tall and mangy looking.

"I hope that you are mistaken!" he said, "and this is not what is in the forest during the day, because they are dangerous and fast. It is speculated that Bigfoots and dog-men do frequent the same forest. Some even believe they are a type of Bigfoot. I don't know that much about them and do not investigate these creatures—but, believe me, you do not want to mess with them, so be very careful if this is what you are dealing with."

I didn't want to tell him that I had already messed with them. I hadn't been very careful sticking the camera in the widow during the day while trying to get photos. Also, the creatures knew of each other because I had seen them together at night.

I regretted not having talked to Mr. Hill sooner about the daytime Bigfoots and their behavior, but again I was apprehensive and confused.

I told him that we hadn't seen anything moving in the forest, so we thought maybe they were gone. He told us to try to stay out of the forest until we knew for sure, and I agreed and hoped they were gone. After I hung up the phone, I felt another form of terror. These creatures knew I was watching them, and my ignorance may have put me in grave danger. Unfortunately, Mr. Hill's advice was too late, and I could do nothing about it.

I was so glad that Mr. Hill never came back to sit in the forest at nightfall. I still get chills thinking about what could have happened to him. At the time I didn't realize that there were other, more dangerous things in the forest. Maybe Mr. Hill was aware of that possibility and that was why he didn't return. He did say he had seen many strange things over the years.

I mentioned this disturbing development only because they might have still been hiding in the forest or they might return. I give this warning to all the Bigfoot investigators out there: if you do find out the location of the forest, just be careful because something else walks upright in these woods.

BIGFOOT NIGHTS
The Nightmare Continues...

By

CHRISTINE D. PARKER
PUBLISHED SOON

Made in the USA
Lexington, KY
13 June 2014